Praise for
The Leader's Playlist

"A leader's primary job is to develop other leaders. To do it right requires emotional intelligence and a willingness to look deep into our own blind spots. Susan Drumm's *The Leader's Playlist* shows in vivid detail the transformation that happens when we are willing to explore what truly holds us back and then honestly deal with it. A remarkable work that should be in every leader's library."

—ROB TARKOFF, executive vice president at Oracle

"Susan Drumm's *The Leader's Playlist* is a wonderful tribute to the need for growth and development for leaders at all levels. It's filled with great research and heartfelt stories of transformation as people learn about themselves and then use what they have learned to scale their organization."

—GREG BROWN, president of Udemy

"An incredible new look at using music to improve our leadership, behavior, and, ultimately, our lives! Susan's concepts are approachable for any reader, backed with the research and experience to leave you equipped with practical knowledge and an understanding of how you can use the psychology to influence every area of your life."

—DR. MARSHALL GOLDSMITH, author of *The Earned Life,*
Triggers, and *What Got You Here Won't Get You There*

"I have always been an advocate for change, both in myself and others. We can't expect people to follow leaders who are not willing to take a long, hard look at ourselves and pivot to be our best every day. As a former violinist and teacher, I also know the amazing transformative power of music. Susan Drumm's *The Leader's Playlist* is both a testament to that power and a handbook for how to use it to be our best selves."

—SHEILA JOHNSON, CEO of Salamander Hotels and Resorts

"As a health-care CEO and one who is passionate about personal growth and healing, I am always on the lookout for new ideas that work. I am delighted to discover Susan Drumm's *The Leader's Playlist*, a book filled from cover to cover with riveting stories of transformation and growth based on the musical playlist we all have running in our heads. She and her team are proving that we can all change for the better if we know how. *The Leader's Playlist* can show you the way. I highly recommend it."

—HUGH LYTLE, founder and CEO of Equality Health

"If you are going to lead and lead well, you are going to have to change your internal playlist. This book will show you how to change the patterns that are getting in your way."

—CAMERON HEROLD, founder of COO Alliance and host of the *Second in Command* podcast

"Small changes can have a disproportionate impact on our future success—but they're not always easy. *The Leader's Playlist* illuminates a powerful path forward: to successfully take action and cue the soundtrack to the life you've always wanted."

—DORIE CLARK, author of *The Long Game* and executive education faculty at Duke University Fuqua School of Business

"Transformation is never easy, but it is impossible unless we start by changing ourselves, the way we see the world, and how we react to it. Susan Drumm's *The Leader's Playlist* is a testament to what can happen when we start with the man (or woman) in the mirror and better understand what brought us here. Inspirational, engaging, and honest. I highly recommend it."

—BILL ADAMS, CEO of the Leadership Circle

"To turn your customers into superfans, your team members need to be the best versions of themselves. Every day. Every interaction. Susan Drumm's *The Leader's Playlist* will help your leaders and teams bring their A game to work and beyond. I highly recommend it!"

—BRITTANY HODAK, speaker and author of *Creating Superfans*

"Susan Drumm's *The Leader's Playlist* confirms what I have always known in my heart: music connects us to each other, the known, and the unknown. Understanding my role in music and applying the lessons I've learned through music have taught me how to be a better leader, manager, partner, and human. Her work proves beyond a shadow of a doubt that it can happen for anyone."

—**BEN JAFFE,** bassist and creative director
of the Preservation Hall Jazz Band

"I believe that music is the language of angels. The power of music has been a study of my entire career. Thank you, Susan, for defining it so wonderfully."

—**BERNIE NELSON,** multiplatinum songwriter for
Kenny Chesney, Wynonna Judd, and others

"A great friend of mine sent me Susan Drumm's new book, *The Leader's Playlist*, and I just finished it. Wow! Where was this book thirty-one years ago, when I moved to Nashville to carve out a career in music? This book completely resonates with and explains insights I have only begun to be aware of in the last few years about how negative experiences as a young child (for me, all the way back to elementary school!) have affected my leadership decisions and professional relationships. I'm no CEO, but I am regularly in charge of teams large and small in the production of film scores and music albums, dealing with directors, artists, players, and studio executives. The use of music and neuroscience in this book to reprogram the negative ways you approach and react to team challenges and life in general is genius! These concepts would have been a huge asset to my career and personal life history. I encourage you to grab it and assimilate it as soon as you possibly can."

—**PAUL MILLS,** composer/mix engineer for *War Room, Woodlawn*, and *Overcomer* and
producer/mixer for Heather Headley, Twila Paris, Don Moen,
Robin Mark, and Phillips, Craig, and Dean

"Susan Drumm is really onto something. As a lifelong songwriter and in my work with veterans with PTSD, I have seen firsthand the correlation between music and healing the past and how finding a new playlist can reset the brain. Bottom line: songs have the power to change us. *The Leader's Playlist* is a groundbreaking work on how this change can happen for leaders in the workplace. I highly recommend it."

—**DAVID LEE,** multiplatinum songwriter of "Letters from Home" (John Michael
Montgomery) and "Lucky Man" (Montgomery Gentry)

"*The Leader's Playlist* is a captivating book in many ways, from its proven ability to help make lasting change to its guidance in creating a powerful playlist that transforms leadership effectiveness and builds personal happiness. Through my work with survivors of some of the worst human atrocities, I can attest to the power of music choices and their use in healing invisible wounds on a more profound level."

—IZABELA LUNDBERG, founder and CEO of Legacy Leaders Institute

"Susan Drumm's new book, *The Leader's Playlist*, confirms what I have always believed about the songs we sing and listen to in our head. The right playlist makes us better. The stories in this book confirm it. Change your playlist, and change your life."

—RUTH KLEIN, business development and writing coach and author of *Time Management Secrets for Working Women* and *Generation Why Not?*

"Susan Drumm's *The Leader's Playlist* shows how even our leadership effectiveness is affected by the past, holding us back with the kind of trapped emotions that have been central to my work in healing others. This book will help you change your playlist and subsequently the choices you make and the level of success you are able to achieve."

—DR. BRADLEY NELSON, author of *The Emotion Code* and creator of the Body Code

"All the evidence is in, and the message is clear. Music, and songs in particular, changes the way we think and how we see ourselves. In her remarkable book, *The Leader's Playlist*, Susan Drumm shares real-life stories of transformation and shows us how the power of songs shapes us as leaders. Hers is a hopeful and positive message based on solid research and experience."

—JILL GRIFFIN, author, speaker, and customer loyalty guru

"Susan Drumm is certainly speaking my language with her new book, *The Leader's Playlist*. Her research and her work with leaders confirm what I have always believed—that none of us can become what we are meant to be in this world without self-awareness and the willingness to change from the inside out. Her message will be music to your ears."

—ALISON WHITMIRE, president of Learning in Action

"In *The Leader's Playlist*, Susan Drumm offers a completely new and fresh idea—a unique take on transformations that works. It's a powerful and hopeful message."

—KAIHAN KRIPPENDORFF, founder of Outthinker and author of *Outthink the Competition*

"I couldn't help but smile and feel joy as I read Susan's wonderfully powerful book. The soundtrack of my childhood resounded in my heart as I made connections and came to understandings about my own journey. Don't just read *The Leader's Playlist*; listen to it in your heart. It will transform your approach to leadership and your life."

—JOE SERIO, PhD, author of *Overcoming Fear: 50 Lessons on Being Bold and Living the Dream*

"In this innovative book, Susan Drumm provides a novel and effective approach to helping leaders transform. She shows how they can break out of old patterns by leveraging the power of music and insights from neurobiology to change outmoded ways of thinking and behaving."

—BEATRICE CHESTNUT, PhD, author of *The Complete Enneagram* and *The 9 Types of Leadership* and coauthor of *The Enneagram Guide to Waking Up*

"I have always believed that success—whatever that looks like for each individual—comes when we get to know ourselves and figure out what we really want in life. Susan Drumm's lovely book, *The Leader's Playlist*, tells us how to act on what we find in that exercise and how to reset our view of the world by changing the music we play in our heads and hearts every day."

—JANELLE BRULAND, author of *The Success Lie: 5 Simple Truths to Overcome Overwhelm and Achieve Peace of Mind*

The Leader's
PLAYLIST

The Leader's
PLAYLIST

UNLEASH THE POWER *of* MUSIC
and NEUROSCIENCE *to* TRANSFORM
YOUR LEADERSHIP *and* YOUR LIFE

SUSAN DRUMM

RIVER GROVE
BOOKS

Published by River Grove Books
Austin, TX
www.rivergrovebooks.com

Distributed by River Grove Books

Design and composition by Greenleaf Book Group
Cover design by Greenleaf Book Group
Cover image: Waveform used under license from Shutterstock.com

Publisher's Cataloging-in-Publication data is available.

Print ISBN: 978-1-63299-601-5

eBook ISBN: 978-1-63299-602-2

First Edition

Contents

Foreword

There are a few books each year that truly catch my attention. *The Leader's Playlist* is one of them. It has been an inspiration to me and my work, as well as an opportunity to reflect on how important a leader's behavior can be in the success of their team and organization, especially in current times.

A blend of well-explained psychology and practical applications for leaders to start using today, this book addresses the heart of leadership behavior while also teaching the powerful shifts you can make to improve your teams, organization, and life now. Susan's research and experience offer a profound guide for how to look at the experiences that shape your behavior and how to get out of toxic patterns and frustrating cycles.

Drawing from compelling studies on music's ability to create new neural pathways, Susan brings a unique element to this process. Breaking out of patterns of triggers for behavior can be difficult, but by creating new systems for your brain to process those stimuli, you can overcome lifelong damaging habits. Learning to hack your brain in this way will create positive results in every area of life: you'll be able to use wider perspectives in decision making, inspire your team around your mission, cultivate deeper personal and professional relationships, and increase productivity and efficiency in the business.

In writing my 2015 book, *Triggers*, I looked at many of the moments that cause us not to be the colleague, partner, parent, or friend we imagine ourselves to be. Environmental triggers cause us to escalate our frustration or irritation and create behaviors that hinder our work, teams, and families. In researching ways to overcome these prompts, I found that the solution was often easy to comprehend but very difficult to do. As *The Leader's Playlist* demonstrates, creating new habits can be something you may feel you know how to do already and may have even attempted before. But without the dedicated implementation of all the strategies presented in the book, it can be easy to fall back into old patterns. Susan walks us through the important process of awareness of our behaviors, recognition of our internal playlist, empowerment to create a new playlist, and ongoing reflection for our progress and understanding of our deeper self.

There has never been a more important time to lead thoughtfully and intentionally than today. My advice is to read this book, start practicing its principles immediately, and watch your leadership and team thrive.

Marshall Goldsmith
Thinkers50 number-one executive coach
Best-selling author of *The Earned Life*, *Triggers*, and *What Got You Here Won't Get You There*

Acknowledgments

I am filled with gratitude for the incredible support of my family, friends, teachers, and clients, all of whom contributed to the creation of this work.

I thank my mother for her drive to make every day count and for her determination to see things through to completion. And for her unending love and support. She is truly my hero.

I am grateful to my big brother and sister, who have been by my side from the beginning. Beverly's compassion, intuition, and deeply empathetic nature are a godsend. I'm so blessed to have her as my sister. David's generosity and love have been foundational to my life. I know I could not have made this journey without him. I thank him for showing me what true masculine unconditional love is.

I also thank one of the greatest teachers of my life, Steven Ringelstein. His love, friendship, coaching, and wisdom are priceless gifts. I hope to carry his message of living in Zone 4—the oneness of love—as my life's work. I am beyond grateful for him.

I thank all those who helped me publish this book, especially Chris Benguhe, who helped me develop the concept and encouraged me to share my story, and Nathan True, who crystalized the messaging behind the music.

I am incredibly blessed to have the support of my Dream Team: Jacqueline Luk Parades, Cory Rogin, and Dierdre Evans. Without their commitment to excellence and unwavering dedication to our mission, this book would not have been possible.

And most of all, I am grateful to Dad. I thank him for being my life's teacher and loving me through his pain. I know he is flying up in Heaven but is still with me energetically every day. I will always love him.

INTRODUCTION

It's Showtime!

This book is about uncovering your internal playlist, the emotional music burned into the deepest recesses of your brain through early life experiences, which directly affects your leadership effectiveness. If something isn't working on the team you're leading, you've come to the right place. I don't know any leader who hasn't struggled in some way in the face of the massive disruption affecting every industry. You may feel you can't retain or engage your people. You may be feeling burnout or that your team is overwhelmed by the pace of change. You may feel that you can't delegate or trust your team to deliver. And yet the only true power you have isn't changing others; it's shifting how you show up as a leader.

When I began my own healing journey, to improve my own leadership and personal outcomes, I turned to music to inspire and soothe me. But it did more than soothe me; I discovered that music could actually heal me. The more I learned about emotional frequencies and the neuroscience behind how music can shift your state of mind, the more I knew I could use this as a turbo drive to help those I coached make the shifts they were yearning to make as well. This isn't just a metaphor. Music has the ability to trigger important synapses in the brain, and it's a powerful access point to understand our behavioral patterns and to create new ones. Music has the ability to help make change stick, by priming the neurological landscape to form new neural pathways in a faster, more efficient way.

You probably aren't aware of how your ingrained reactions affect the people and relationships around you, including how you lead. If you aren't aware of what is happening, you have no power to access and change it. By connecting the defining moments of your life to specific emotions you were feeling, you can identify how and why you react to similar emotions now. Interesting patterns emerge. These patterns are your default playlist. They're the soundtrack of your behavior. Of course, consciously, none of us would choose to create some of the difficult or damaging experiences we live through, such as confrontations or failures at work and in life. But we each have a pattern of experiences and emotions that plays out over and over; like that annoying song stuck in our head, our unconscious playlist is stuck on repeat. If our playlist keeps playing the same songs, bringing up the same emotions and experiences, why not just choose a new playlist?

But first, as I discovered this process, I had to get really clear on exactly what was on the old playlist. I had to let go of judgment about how and why it was created. How and why don't really matter at the end of the day, but they can help you understand your playlist's origin. I identified the songs that represented the repeated emotional experiences I was generating in different circumstances in my life. This was a critical step, because once you do this work, you are far more conscious of when you are triggered and back on the eight-lane highway to hell. You catch yourself early and take the first exit. But you also need to know where to find the exit, and that is where the new playlist becomes central.

If you could create a new playlist, what songs—and the emotions they trigger—would you want on that playlist? That's what I created, literally and figuratively. I burned these new songs into memory, generating the emotional experiences I was seeking, such as feeling blessed and loved. I learned that I didn't need the external world to give this to me. I had to create it in my internal world.

And as I did this, both my work and my personal relationships transformed, so that the external world mirrored my new playlist. I could be more present with the people I loved, show more empathy, and inspire them just with my way of being. And I attracted new relationships into my life that reflected back to me the songs that were now stuck in my head. Rather than thinking going on a meditation retreat was something I "should" do (read: stick-a-needle-in-my-eye kind of fun), I now couldn't wait to experience this type of retreat. And as I opened up to that, I met extraordinary leaders and friends whose playlists resonated more with my upgraded version. They say you are the company you keep, and naturally as my playlist upgraded, my relationships did as well. "Healer, heal thyself."

The benefits were not only to my personal life but to my professional life as well. I attracted extraordinary clients into my practice because I showed up differently as a coach. I had a deeper level of warmth *and* strength to help facilitate these leaders' evolutions. What I was specifically able to do is to see the playlist within them and help them see it too. With awareness, they had a greater power to change.

I had walked the path I invited them to walk, and that level of authenticity speaks volumes. I didn't treat them as "clients," and I wouldn't tolerate being treated as a "vendor." I engaged with billionaire clients as equals, because they were, and that's not the energy level others in their life tend to show up with. I approached them the same way I coached the yoga studio owner and the graphic designer. Each had their own signature playlist, and my mission was to help them hear it and shift the parts that needed to be shifted to bring greater self-love and empathy for others.

As their internal landscape shifted, so too did their external landscape: deeper relationships at work and home, improved health and sleep, and an ability to scale their organization in a way they had not been able to tap into before. They are ordinary and extraordinary. And so are you.

In this book, I share a process that I used for myself and the executives I coach for leadership evolution. The executives' names have been changed to protect their privacy, and many of the details have been combined or reimagined to serve as better examples, but the principles and benefits are all real.

I've been leveraging the Enneagram in my coaching work for almost a decade. As applied to leadership development, it is a model of human psychology that identifies an executive's core leadership style within a set of interconnected personality types. In short, there isn't just one type of "great" leadership. Leaders lead in different ways and have their own natural styles. Understanding your leadership style is incredibly helpful within the model of the Enneagram, because it points to the areas where you most need to grow to be a better leader. In other words, understanding your own leadership style will illuminate the path of development specifically for *you.*

The Enneagram influenced the way I saw what propelled leaders forward and what held them back. It also got me intrigued about how the human brain works and where these different leadership gifts and blind spots come from. Although we are all unique and face unique problems, I noticed that we tend to react to triggering events in a limited number of ways, or a set pattern, as I saw after coaching leaders for twenty years. And I noticed some commonality in childhood experiences with leaders of the same leadership style.

This helped me create my own process for coaching executives, looking at the core wound that affects their leadership and their life and developing strategies to shift it. If you know the Enneagram well, you will see some connections in how I describe the wound, or old playlist, with different Enneagram types. What I've identified are the nine most common playlists I've seen, born out of childhood wounds, that are influencing leaders today. But it's not a one-to-one match with the Enneagram, as I'd like people to feel free to describe their own playlist in the way that feels accurate to them. Use what I've provided here as guidance and inspiration, focusing on naming your own playlist and following the path to enlightened leadership.

Using research on neuroscience-based leadership techniques, this process harnesses left- and right-brain thinking to make lasting changes in how you think and how you view the world. As with any change, if you revert to your old behavior or way of thinking, you may struggle, but you will have the steps needed to dust yourself off and pick up where you left off.

You first need to get clear on your intentions. What are you no longer willing to tolerate in your life? You must be willing to focus your efforts to build new neural pathways. It will require a deeper level of curiosity than you may have ever thought to use to understand why certain experiences trigger certain reactions in you or why certain emotional patterns show up in your life. I walk you through identifying your current playlist of emotional experiences that are running in the background of your life. You'll understand how that behavioral pattern may be getting in the way of creating what you want. You will uncover how your childhood experiences determined the songs on the playlist, and you'll find uncanny links between what happened to you way back then and what's happening to you now. Your emotions carry specific frequencies, like the frequencies of music, and you'll learn the tools to create a new, more empowering playlist than the one that was grooved into your brain long ago. With newfound freedom from the weight of the old playlist, you will unleash energy to focus on a meaningful mission that ultimately provides more joy and happiness than running from your past.

My work is to help the leader hear that playlist and understand how it has influenced their life and their leadership. With that new awareness comes the opportunity to heal wounds, bringing on the empowerment to create a new playlist and ultimately focus on something to help humanity rather than inflicting further wounds on the next generation, as well as on themselves.

When I work with teams, I see a range of reactions from the individual members of those teams. Some of them are hungry for development. They communicate effectively what they need, and they know what doesn't work for them or for the success of the team. Some are less ready to take on the challenge. After working with more than a hundred teams, I've noticed an interesting pattern. How far and how fast these leaders develop is a bell curve. Those who really are curious about themselves (interested in development and not afraid to look in the mirror) have the greatest transformation in awareness and ultimately happiness. That's about 25 percent of the team. There is a middle 50–60 percent who achieve some personal breakthroughs. There is definitely improvement in their leadership, but they are not quite ready for transformation.

Then there is the bottom 20 percent. Inevitably, two leaders out of a ten-person team will resist any sort of development, and me holding up the mirror for them will only trigger them to react defensively or to avoid the process. It is too scary to the ego to get curious and look at their own patterns. Instead, they might complain to the CEO about this "team development bullshit" or even actively sabotage the coaching process for their team. They openly or subversively attack the project. Almost always, they project the views that "my shit don't stink" and "we need to focus on 'real work.'" My job is to hold up the mirror, gather feedback, and have the leader take a deeper look at how they are showing up. I need to be courageous in doing so, but I need you to be courageous too.

Leaders who are reluctant to change likely provide some kind of value to their teams (or else they would have been fired). But someone unwilling to change is likely to have a difficult time collaborating with the rest of the team. Notice the correlation: Those leaders who exemplify "I'm resistant to growing and developing" embody in the same way "I'm resistant to hearing feedback from and working more collaboratively with my peers." It has nothing to do with the work itself. It has everything to do with the playlist running them. That playlist was created long ago in their childhood, and it makes them feel too threatened to look at themselves in the mirror.

If you haven't invested in the self-reflection to understand the playlist that is running you, the results you produce in your life will be limited by the perspectives you burned into your brain as a child. Frankly, this is an important message for any human, not just the senior leaders I work with. But since my playground is working with senior leaders, I most want you to hear this message because the quality of your leadership affects others. This effect is compounded if you lead a larger department or organization.

Because we can't rely on government to efficiently solve our societal and economic challenges, our corporate leaders are often the ones who are either improving the human condition or worsening it. The decisions and choices of a highly conscious leader will be different from those of an unconscious one who is being run by an ego-based, flight-or-fight playlist. And underneath it all, when you are choosing a more empowered and conscious playlist as the backdrop for your leadership, the best talent will flock to work with you. If I, as your employee, am working with a motivated and compelling leader who is committed to a meaningful mission outside their egoistic needs, my work becomes more of a joy. And when I walk through that door at night and greet my children, while I may be tired, I am inspired.

I wrote this book in response to the pain of so many younger leaders who yearn for true leadership but experience very few examples in business (and, frankly, politics as well). I wrote this book for the senior leaders who also yearn to get off the hamster wheel of their triggers and wounds and want to evolve to a higher level of consciousness and enlightenment. I wrote it for the children of these same leaders, so they could experience a parent who doesn't project his or her wounds onto the next generation.

I'm fully engaged in helping CEOs build awareness about how their childhood wounds affect their current leadership. My goal is to empower them to change their own playlist to something far more enlightening. I target CEOs and their leadership teams because now that their ambition has driven them to lead organizations, they are ripe for the next level of growth in *how* they lead. In terms of Maslow's hierarchy of needs, they generally have their basic needs (physiological and safety needs) and even their esteem and belonging needs met.[1] It's the need for self-actualization, the top of the pyramid, that many are hungry for and find elusive. In addition, at the CEO level, we have the most leverage for shifting culture and enhancing performance, but leaders at this level can often be the hardest to convince to change. It is crucial, now more than ever, that the change start at the top.

CEOs and senior executives who read this book and invest the time into uncovering their inner workings can free themselves from their childhood wounds. At this level, you likely have at least three or four layers of management, and as a senior executive, you are not as close to the front line of doing the work as you may have been at the organization's inception. Now, getting things done through others becomes paramount, and how you show up in relationship to others determines your level of success. Our childhood wounds are most likely to be triggered in managing relationships and collaborating with others. If we haven't done the work to heal these aspects of ourselves, they are exposed while we try to run the marathon of scaling an organization. But when you do the work of healing yourself, the ripple effect in the organization can be transformational.

Sadly, many entrepreneurs are too busy "doing" and haven't yet had a bellyful of their own destructive or reactive behavior. They simply aren't ready to invest in themselves at this point, choosing instead to focus on pouring their energy into the business and believing that they don't have the time for this work, since they are just trying to survive. Only after they achieve some level of success are they willing to open the door to heal their wounds. That's when they begin to realize that the success they thought would bring them happiness and peace turns out to be a mirage. They are still fighting demons—those demons keep following them. These entrepreneurs eventually realize that, if they truly want to experience joy and peace in their lives, they are going to have to turn and face the monster.

The younger generations tend to be more open to introspection and hungry for breakthroughs that will help them rise to higher positions of leadership. Their curiosity and growth mindset are the tinder that helps ignite true transformation. For these individuals, there's less difficulty convincing them that their childhood wounds may hold them back.

These true rising stars know that, to advance professionally, they need to do the inner work to heal so they can be free to commit to a meaningful mission that doesn't involve feeding their wound. Though this generation may have its faults and its challenges, openness is its strength.

Now is the time for this level of transformation in our leadership. In the United States, our nation is divided, and we are challenged to find empathy for those with opposing viewpoints. Across the world, political leaders continue to attack each other and lead from a highly wounded perspective of power and control. The impact of poor leadership on our planet is palpable; the greed and unending consumption is literally creating a meltdown of our environment. The answer does not lie in controlling or governing others as much as we would like it to be. The answer lies in healing ourselves so we may inspire others to heal. As wonderfully stated by the emotional intelligence experts at Learning in Action, healing the divide within us will heal the divide between us.[2]

The bottom line is that your personal evolution *is* your leadership transformation. You might think transformation suggests that growth happens in an instant, like the butterfly magically appearing from the cocoon. What you didn't see is all the work inside the cocoon to have it evolve to the butterfly. Evolution takes place over a period of time with focused effort. Otherwise, the old playlist, the old neural pathways, will continue to have their way with you. Some people are still searching for that magic, fat-burning pill to go from fat to skinny, but the reality is that it takes consistency of focus to change to a new habit with a new mindset to transform the body.

This isn't a magic-pill leadership book. It's a how-to-bring-out-magic-in-*you* leadership book. It is important that we, as humans, start the evolving process now. Our current level of hatred, divisiveness, exuberant consumption, socioeconomic disparity, and climate crisis demands that we stop trying to fix the world around us and do the work to shift the internal landscape. We can't shift the external landscape until we shift the internal landscape. In reality, this book applies to all people, but it's a leadership book because those in power are the biggest point of leverage for change.

It's my hope that the vulnerability with which I share my story, as well as the stories of others I have coached, will inspire you to follow the inspiration of Michael Jackson's "Man in the Mirror": if you want to make the world a better place, you need to look within and change yourself first. We need more kindness, empathy, tolerance, patience, confidence, enthusiasm, and joy in our world. So I ask you: How often are you feeling those emotions in your inner world? Have you had a bellyful of reactivity or have a deep enough curiosity to look at the divisiveness, fear, and anxiety in yourself?

Childhood Trauma and Business Leadership

There is no way of denying the pain and suffering that happens to so many of us as children. Our upbringings might have seemed typical and normal from the outside, and even to us, but upon closer view, they might have scarred us tremendously. We need to stop being afraid to open the door of discovery—not to linger in that room but to use it as a passageway.

Significant traumas, such as physical abuse by a parent or the death of a parent when you were a young child, can have a massive effect on you as a functioning adult. I didn't suffer in these dramatic ways, but I had my own wounding moments, when the fight-or-flight response was triggered and the neuron synapses became deeply grooved as a result of my fear. We have all had traumas or wounds of some sort—some far worse than others, but this isn't a contest. After coaching leaders for almost twenty years, here's what I know: *whatever your personal childhood wounds are, they affect your leadership today.* In my role as a leadership coach, I have seen leaders react to the same situations in very different ways. What makes some leaders able to handle stressful situations more gracefully, while others get their buttons pushed and become reactive?

In the book *Childhood Disrupted,* Donna Jackson Nakazawa describes how our childhood traumas, wounds, and stresses can change our brain and body chemistry, causing physical and mental health challenges. She details story after story in which parental emotional or physical abuse gets lodged in the psyche and eventually manifests itself in illnesses such as multiple sclerosis (MS), severe migraines, Crohn's disease, and cancer. This may seem like a coincidence until you see the numerous studies that link adverse childhood events to physical and mental health issues that may appear twenty, thirty, and even forty years later. Nakazawa writes, "According to neurobiologists who study childhood adversity, children from unhappy, dysfunctional families who experience chronic adversity undergo changes in brain architecture that create lasting physical scars."[1]

Toxic stress changes our brains. When we are stressed, adrenaline and cortisol course through our veins and trigger immune cells to whip our bodies into a fight-or-flight response. When you have a healthy stress response, you are able to return to calmness immediately after the danger has passed. But sometimes the stress response is so frequently or significantly triggered that the memory gets deeply encoded in the brain. This causes the brain to be on perpetual high alert, looking for similar threats.

Emotions cause a physical response in the body. Our chests can literally hurt after a significant breakup. When we are nervous before speaking in front of a large crowd, our palms get sweaty, or we can feel sick to our stomachs. As Nakazawa shares, there is a powerful connection between our mental stress and emotions. When your system is repeatedly exposed to stress, your stress response—and the hormones associated with it—are always on, secreting inflammatory chemicals into the body that damage tissue over time. Inflammation translates into disease, which is why the studies show that, for example, if you lose an adult sibling, your risk of having a heart attack rises greatly. A child's death triples the chance of a parent developing MS. Children whose parents divorce are far more likely to have strokes as adults.[2]

Research regarding the effect of stress on early brain development is illuminating. "Early stress causes changes in the brain," Nakazawa writes, "that reset the immune system so that you no longer respond to stress or . . . respond to stress in an exacerbated way."[3] This change to our lifelong stress response happens through epigenetic modifications—by which both good and bad influences on our developing brain alter which of our genes become active. Some of these genes are the ones that influence our stress response in the brain, including those that downregulate stress to allow our bodies to return to homeostasis. As Nakazawa puts it, "Early childhood stress biologically reprograms how we will react to stressful events for our entire lives."[4] What's more, we often don't see the link as adults; we don't understand why we are triggered or responding in the way that we are. Our responses to workplace events can be traced back to childhood stress. That stress response becomes the water we swim in, and it seems normal to us.

There is an important difference in the types of stress that have a lasting effect on our brain chemistry. Studies show that unpredictable stress, such as a volatile parent, or multiple emotional shocks, have far more damaging impacts on our stress response and mental health than does predictable stress, such as dealing with food shortages during winter months. If the stressor happens in the same way at the same time, children don't show the same types of lasting epigenetic changes as those whose environment creates unpredictable stress.[5]

This research can be used to understand the wound that may have affected and altered your own response to stress. What unpredictable events took place for you growing up, and how did they shape you? What recent events have triggered you—and what aspect of those recent events made them similar to the unpredictable events that you experienced as a child?

Repeating Behavior

My father was a skilled dentist, but he hated it and was resentful. He had always wanted to be a pilot. However, he was so intelligent that my grandmother thought it would be a waste for him to just fly planes. She argued that he should make his family proud by being a doctor. He felt that my grandma pushed him into dental school, and despite graduating with honors, he never overcame the disappointment.

That perspective had massive impact on the whole family. Although my dad had a successful practice, he would spend money on cars, boats, motor homes, and other expensive toys to distract himself from the pain he felt from going to work every day. He invested in get-rich-quick schemes at every turn, in the hopes that it would save him from life as a dentist. This created a lot of conflict between him and my mother. We lived well, but they had no savings to cover emergencies or for retirement, and Dad kept looking for a way out.

Dad would come home from work in a miserable state. He would storm into the house and go straight to the recliner, expecting my mom to wait on him, bring him his soda, and get dinner on the table. When he came in, sometimes he was so mired in frustration, he wouldn't even say hello. One time, he came in while I was watching TV. He plopped into his chair and changed the channel.

I said, "Hi, Dad. I was watching that program."

His response was to yell, "Get out!"

That was pretty tough for a six-year-old to hear from her father. At times like these, I felt ignored and insignificant, as if I didn't matter at all. Our entire household seemed to be centered on placating Dad. Dad made the money—and he suffered for us by staying in the career he hated—so we had better do everything as he wished.

I think this is why I developed a low tolerance for suffering in a job I don't like doing. It explains a lot of the twists and turns in my career path. For instance, while I loved the study of law, I dreaded graduating from law school and going to work in a large law firm. I had split both my summer internships, working for four different law firms and getting a taste of different types of law: litigation, securities, labor, and employment. I hoped that one of these specializations would get me more fired up to do the job that I had just spent three years studying and in which I had invested over $100,000 in education costs (back in the early 1990s!). But all I could see was that the two-year associate was unhappy, the five-year associate was miserable, and the partner seemed happy but only because they had financial success.

My days would be spent researching and writing briefs and memorandums the first several years, and it felt like going to prison. I felt trapped. I had to make at least $80,000 a year upon graduation to pay off the loans, but I didn't want to enslave myself to working ninety hours a week in a job I wasn't the least bit excited about.

Faced with the potential of being miserable like my dad, I was forced to get creative. I started looking into management consulting. Fortunately, my timing was perfect. That was the first year that management consulting firms like McKinsey and the Boston Consulting Group (BCG) came to law school campuses to be part of the recruiting season along with law firms. After a long interview process, I jumped for joy, skipping down the pavement, when I landed a job working for BCG. I wouldn't have to be miserable doing law. I wouldn't be going down my father's path. Ah, what freedom!

But, like many things, sometimes the reality doesn't quite live up to the dream. I'd learn later that this had more to do with me than with the job. Whatever your personal wound is, it keeps following you until you heal it. Repeating a behavior induced by a childhood wound will bring about the same results each time—physically and emotionally—in your life, your relationships, and your work.

PTSD

In the book *The Body Keeps the Score: Brain, Mind, and Body in the Healing of Trauma*, author Bessel van der Kolk writes, "We have learned that trauma is not just an event that took place sometime in the past; it is also the imprint left by that experience on the mind, brain, and body. The imprint has ongoing consequences for how the human organism manages to survive in the present."[6]

He goes on to describe in vivid detail the neurobiology of traumatic stress, through his research with patients suffering from post-traumatic stress disorder (PTSD). You see, ideally our stress hormone system should provide a quick response to move us away from perceived danger and then return to equilibrium. However, in PTSD patients, the hormonal system fails at returning the body to status, and the fight, flight, or freeze signals continue after the danger is over. This continued secretion of stress hormones wreaks havoc on our long-term health. Van der Kolk's studies show that, when traumatized people are presented with images, sounds, or thoughts related to their experience, the amygdala lights up with a fear response even decades after the initial event.

The brain scans of these patients revealed that, during these flashbacks, only the right side of the brain would light up. Additional research into brain function shows that the different hemispheres of the brain perform different functions. The right is "intuitive, emotional, visual, and tactical, while the left is linguistic, sequential, and analytical."[7] What this means is that when someone reminds traumatized people of the past, "their right brain reacts as if the traumatized event were happening in the present." Given that the left brain isn't firing during these experiences, they may not realize that they are "reexperiencing and reenacting the past; they are just furious, terrified, enraged, ashamed, or frozen."[8]

The ability to detect danger is critically important to our survival, and the oldest part of the brain, the amygdala, has a central role in releasing cortisol and adrenaline to prepare us to survive. The amygdala relies on another part of the brain, the medial prefrontal cortex (MPFC), which is located directly above our eyes, to read the danger signals and assess whether a threat is credible. For traumatized individuals, van der Kolk's studies show that activity in the MPFC is significantly reduced, such that the amygdala is overactivated. "When the system breaks down, we become like conditioned animals: The moment we detect danger, we automatically go into fight or flight mode."[9]

Van der Kolk highlights two ways to create a better balance or communication between the MPFC and the amygdala: The first is to strengthen the capacity of the MPFC to monitor body sensations. We can do this through meditation and yoga. The second is to recalibrate the nervous system to respond to external stimuli. We can access that through breath, movement, touch—or sound.

According to van der Kolk, the key to stable mental health and physical health is learning to live in the present. But that is awfully hard to do when your reactions are encoded from childhood trauma that continually draws you back into experiences where you relive the wound.

Earliest Trauma

One of the wounds I frequently relived happened when I was two or three years old. According to my mother, I was a highly energetic child, who always wanted to play, play, play, and I would go after the joy of play with gusto. So it's no surprise I acted the way I did when I saw my brother and his friend playing with his Matchbox cars in our basement. My brother Dave was five years older than me, and I loved him, although I'm sure at that young age, I was a pesky little sister. I wanted to join in his fun and play with the cars too, but, of course, he was having none of it. They were his, and he was with his friend, and I was too young to play with cars like these. Somehow I pulled at the Matchbox car box, and all the cars went flying around the room. My brother burst into tears in frustration.

He ran upstairs, and the next thing I heard was my father's pounding footsteps. He came barreling down the stairs in extreme anger—directed at me. He towered over me and screamed. I don't remember what he said. All I can remember is the extreme fear I felt. And I can still access the fear that I felt at the time. Terrified, I ran up the stairs and felt him chasing me. For all I knew, I was running in fear for my life and needed to get away as quickly as I could.

It was my first experience of my father's wrath, which I would later see many times over. He was a big man: 6'2" with a large build and an intensity to match. When he was angry, his whole face turned red, and his eyes bulged out of his head. But up to this particular point, I had only known my father as a loving daddy. My mother always said he had a special bond with me when I was born. Of his three kids, I was the first that he was willing to change a diaper for. Most likely it was because he was older by the time I came onto the scene and he was a bit more interested in parenting. I've seen plenty of photos where he hoisted me up onto his chest and held me in the crook of his arm, both of us happy.

It's hard for me to describe just how intense my father's anger could be. Later in life, I'd see him make grown people cry. His sudden and terrifying anger could seemingly come from nowhere. It's as if an alien took him over during these episodes. To be the target of his wrath was terrifying to everyone in my family, and we were all a target at some point.

I ran behind the couch and hid, weeping and shaking. My mother eventually coaxed me out. By this point, my father had calmed down and felt bad about what he did, so he wanted to do something nice for me. I had a voracious sweet tooth, and he knew it. So, he made a me a snow cone. Once he produced the bright red cone, he sat down in his lounge chair. He called me over. Prodded by my mother, I did as I was told, climbing up onto his lap. I ate the snow cone while still sobbing, gasping for air in between each lick.

This type of experience—and we have all had a traumatic childhood experience—lives in the brain and body as a deep marker for creating our fight-or-flight response. I remember feeling betrayed, and perhaps even a feeling of righteousness. Even as a very young child, I thought, *You think a snow cone makes up for what you just did?* I knew I didn't deserve to be treated that way, but I had to bury this feeling deep inside me and pretend everything was okay to continue to survive in my household. It was a secret resentment; one in which my subconscious would be highly attuned to in any situation where I felt betrayed or like I was being treated unfairly.

21

That resentment has come back to visit many times in my life—at work, in my relationships, any time I feel attacked. Eventually, I categorized the feelings associated with this early trauma that resurface with each of those adult confrontations:

- Feeling left out: I wanted to be included with my brother's play, but I was shunned.

- Feeling treated unfairly: My father's wrath was vastly overblown for what had actually occurred.

- Feeling frustration: The root cause of this frustration is the resentment and betrayal I felt at the core.

Until I could clearly see that initial wound, I was unable to see how my professional and personal behavior fed off it. Tracing it back to its inception proved hugely valuable because until you can see it, you can't manage it. The work I've done most recently is to understand and value why the reaction to that wound was created in the first place and how it served (or hoped) to protect me. However, it also kept creating experiences in my life where I would feel the same emotions.

Superpower

I have much compassion and love for my father, especially now. He wasn't all bad—not at all. I knew he was proud of me and deeply loved me, and I loved him. When I was a teenager, he took a keen interest in my athletic ability and went to every track meet I competed in to cheer me on, shouting, "Run, Susie, run!" As an adult, my dad continued to encourage me in my business by sharing stories and quips that I could use in my speeches. He wasn't a dark character by any means; it was more that he was unpredictable. His wrath might show up at any time, and that wrath was born out of his own childhood wounds.

Today I'm grateful for everything I experienced. I learned at a young age to read his moods so I knew how to handle him. It's a skill I honed to such perfection that it has formed the basis of the work I do today. I have to intently focus on others and read them in a way that goes beyond what most people can do, so that I can truly coach them effectively. I don't think I would be able to do my work if I hadn't needed to develop that skill as a survival technique. Despite the trauma of having a volatile father, the gift of the experience has been extraordinary.

For each wound, there is a strength or a gift that develops as a direct result of that wound. It gives us our superpower in leadership. For me, it was the ability to read people closely and develop my emotional quotient (EQ), or emotional intelligence, to create safety within relationships. Had I not had to watch my father's behavior closely, look for signs of his volatile wrath, and even help de-escalate conflict if I saw warning signs, I would not have honed this skill to such a degree that it made being a CEO coach a great fit for my talents.

You likely have your own leadership superpower. Do you have a creative vision that leads to innovation? Are you able to inspire others or set them at ease? Are you extremely versatile or able to adapt to sudden change and market upheaval? That superpower likely has its roots in your upbringing, possibly in an emotional wound. If you can look at your wound as providing you with your superpower, then you have less judgment of yourself about the wound itself.

The Frequency of the Heart

In many of my early jobs, I felt mistreated. I was frustrated by the situation, wanting so much to break out of the cycle, but I didn't realize yet what that cycle was. Looking back, I can see that I was just reacting to the events of life; I was certainly not responding from an elevated place of wisdom. I had dreams and expectations, and every time those were dashed, I would go into a pattern of victimhood for being treated unfairly. In situations like this, you can retreat further into a victim mindset, or you can dig deeper to understand how you are the author of your experiences.

I came to understand from my courses, certifications, and research on neuroscience and the brain-body connection that, fundamentally, we are energetic beings. Particularly impactful was the research published by the HeartMath Institute (available at heartmath.org). The heart is the largest source of electricity in our body. The electricity it produces can be picked up by an electroencephalogram (EEG), a test that detects electrical activity in the brain. It is so powerful that the heartbeat generates an electromagnetic signal that can be measured three feet out from the body. The brain also produces electricity, but its signal is weaker and can be measured only to about an inch from the body.

We emit an electromagnetic signal, a wave with a certain frequency. Spectral analysis techniques show that information about our emotional state is encoded in our heart's magnetic field. Just like when you tune your radio, you are able to pick up various frequencies or stations. You can't see the frequency, but you know it's there when the music comes through loud and clear. Each of us is broadcasting information about what we are feeling, and that signal affects others around us, whether or not we are conscious of it. And we are also subconsciously picking up the signals of others.

When we react in the same way to events in our lives over and over, it is because we are hearing the same frequency broadcasting the same message. The frequency you broadcast, subconsciously or not, is also what returns to you. Emotions such as anger, jealousy, and shame have lower frequencies than emotions such as compassion, gratitude, and love. What's more, emotions are either renewing our bodies (hormonally, with the aid of the autonomic nervous system) or depleting our energy.

As much as it felt like life was happening to me when I felt those familiar patterns of being left out, frustrated, and treated unfairly, what I didn't realize was that these reactions were a favorite radio frequency of mine, playing the same songs over and over again. The brain likes familiarity, and this was a station I knew well, so my brain kept on broadcasting it.

Of course I didn't want to be playing these songs, and I would be angry at life, God, or whomever I saw as the source of my pain. And that pattern is likely to return to the same song in the next go-round. *I must get off the merry-go-round*, I vowed. To do that, I had to see that my childhood experiences hardwired a neural pathway in my brain for these emotions. I could indeed jump off the merry-go-round and set myself free.

What if we can change the station? Even better, what if we take control of the songs that are played? Instead of a radio, let's think of it as a playlist. Our wounds start playing songs of hurt, anger, and fear. Those songs are catchy, but they lead to unproductive or even destructive reactions at work and at home. The songs get stuck in our head, and the playlist is perpetually on repeat in the background. In order to heal our wounds, we need to change those songs, create a new playlist. We need to replace our wounded playlist with songs of love, empathy, and empowerment.

A New Playlist for a New Type of Leader

Everyone is unique, and there are clearly countless playlists that could be running inside you. In my years of coaching, I have come across several that keep popping up and plaguing business leaders.

The meaningful mission behind this work is helping leaders lead in a way that brings out the best in others. When you understand what you are running from and have the tools to shift the old playlist running your life, you will be able to focus on what really matters to you. You'll make better decisions by widening your perception and seeing what is really happening in the moment instead of filtering data based on old neural pathways. Ultimately, running toward something is far more inspiring than running away from something. You'll find that you attract others who are as committed as you are to a meaningful mission. These people become loyal to you and the vision you create. Leaders often notice that their business scales more efficiently when they are more effective at influencing and inspiring others rather than defending, protecting, controlling, or coping. Personal and work relationships become deeper and more meaningful, driving a culture that attracts and retains top-level talent.

Before you see the external world shift in how it responds to you, you will feel a shift internally. You'll notice that you stop exhausting yourself trying *not* to be like someone else (likely one or both of your parents) and instead feel more accepting of and loving toward who you actually are. You let go of the illusion of control and are able to create what you want with greater ease and joy. I see leaders become more resilient, have more fun, and inspire people just by their way of being. And *then* the external world responds to that!

You are essentially becoming a new type of leader. Those who recognize that the old style of leadership simply doesn't work in today's disruptive, escalating rate-of-change environment are enlightened to find a better, healthier way to lead. If you walk the path toward enlightened leadership and overcome your wounds, you are less reactive to others (whom you can't control anyway) and more interested in leading from a place of making a positive difference for others. Rather than running from or trying to avoid feeling the wound, which inevitably sends out the frequency that will result in inadvertently triggering the wound, you instead put your attention on a mission that is greater than you. At its core, this mission will be based on love rather than fear, and your ambition and drive will be rooted in improving the lives and conditions of the stakeholders you care about. We cannot lead how we led in the past, in the ego-dominated "What is truth?" era. Leaders who try to hold on to the old model of leading simply struggle to stay relevant and keep the next generation engaged. Instead, heal your wound, change your playlist, and become an enlightened leader.

2

The Power of Music

An enormous body of research indicates that music is one of the most powerful tools you can use to increase *neuroplasticity*—or wiring new neural pathways in the brain. When you listen to your favorite song, you may experience the same high you would from eating chocolate or having great sex. In this book, we use the power of music in two ways. First, we use it to clarify when an old neural pathway, one that we have determined no longer works for us, is activated. Second, we use music to help us strengthen a new neural pathway, one that we want to replace the old one with.

Joel Beckerman, author of *The Sonic Boom: How Sound Transforms the Way We Think, Feel, and Buy* speaks to the power that music has to influence human beings to a more desired emotional state: "Sound has surprising power to influence our decisions, opinions, and actions in ways we might not even notice. . . . The key to an effective sonic strategy is the creation of . . . transcendent instants when sound connects with a listener's emotional core."[1]

Beckerman's organization, Made Music Studio, was involved in a workplace study to see if the innovative use of sound could increase productivity. Office workers were connected to sensors that gathered biometric data. After listening to different auditory stimuli, they were required to complete motor skills and comprehension tests to see how well they retained information.

The test involved four different types of "music," which the workers listened to through headphones: The first type was no music or sound at all. This was meant to represent a normal workplace setting. The second type was ambient music, similar to spa music. Next was "entrainment," ambient music with a low frequency pulse that would gradually slow in tempo. This pulse was intended to subliminally train the heart to beat at a lower rate. The final type was dynamic. In this case, the listener heard the entrainment music again with the pulse. However, based on the listener's heart rate, the pulse would vary in tempo. If the listener's heart rate was too fast, the pulse would slow down; if their heart rate was too slow (which might mean they were falling asleep), the pulse would speed up.

In terms of productivity, the researchers found that the dynamic condition was the most effective. By actively using music to help control the listener's heart rate, Beckerman and his team could bring the listener to an optimal state of focus. Their tests showed the highest levels of productivity in this state. If the person was experiencing anxiety, the music helped slow their heart rate down to relax them; if the person was too relaxed (sleepy), it would energize them.

Music has the power to alter our mood and emotional feelings, via direct release of dopamine to the brain. Listening to music also produces oxytocin, increasing empathy, understanding, and compassion while enabling us to get in deeper touch with our emotions. It also can reduce stress and anxiety, which interrupts symptoms of depression. It improves attention, which helps the brain anticipate events. Music also releases endorphins, which ease pain and stabilize the immune system, and it improves the quality of sleep, which also reduces depression.[2]

Consider the research on music and the brain during exercise. When we exercise, our body starts sending messages to take a break because it just feels easier to sit on the couch. However, music competes for our brain's attention, enabling us to push through mild fatigue. What's more, it can help us use our energy more efficiently. In a recent study, it was found that cyclists listening to music require 7 percent less oxygen than those who did not.[3]

Since 2006, two University of Central Florida professors, neuroscientist Kiminobu Sugaya and world-renowned violinist Ayako Yonetani, have been teaching one of the most popular courses at the university. "Music and the Brain" explores how music affects brain function and human behavior.

"Usually, in the late stages, Alzheimer's patients are unresponsive," Sugaya says. "But once you put on the headphones that play [their favorite] music, their eyes light up. They start moving and sometimes singing. The effect lasts maybe 10 minutes or so even after you turn off the music." This can be seen on an MRI, where "lots of different parts of the brain light up."[4] As reported on the website of Dementia Care Central, in one study of late-stage dementia patients, listening to twenty minutes of music resulted in an immediate, measurable increase in happiness, eye contact, and talkativeness and a decrease in fatigue. Neuroscientists have described the effect of music on subjects with dementia as "lifting the haze."[5]

The impact of music on the brain occurs right from the very start. A recent Carnegie Hall article, "Why Making Music Matters," shares Dr.

Dennie Wolf's research findings that day-old infants breathe differently depending on whether they are listening to Mozart or Stravinsky, that music soothes premature babies (and their worried parents) in hospital nurseries, and that babies will listen calmly to a lullaby for twice as long as baby talk or adult speech.[6]

Changing the music you listen to can have profound effects on your mood. It can even be used to train your brain to feel different emotions. Changing your mental playlist from sad songs about loss and rejection to empowering songs about success and wonder can drastically change your outlook on life, work, and relationships.

There are many songs that made up my old playlist of feeling left out, treated unfairly, frustrated, and betrayed, just as you have multiple songs in your playlist. Listening to certain songs helps me give a voice to my emotions. One representative song for me is "Jar of Hearts" by Christina Perri, which features a deeply emotionally scarred woman singing of her pain from a breakup. As John Hill of About.com said of the song, "There have been countless 'you did me wrong' songs through the history of pop music, but identifying a serial dater as a collector of broken hearts is one of the more unique ways of displaying both hurt and frustration."[7] When I was going through my divorce, listening to that song was a way I could connect to the emotions I was feeling.

However, there is a difference between feeling and identifying the emotion and holding on to the emotion. Holding onto negative emotions, repeating those feelings over and over, gets us into trouble by creating deeply grooved pathways in our brain. We are not always aware of holding on to emotion; identifying the emotional playlist helps us become conscious of that groove, and we can make a shift to something else.

I know which song turned it around for me. It was "24K Magic," by Bruno Mars, and it was the perfect antidote. I love Bruno Mars's energy. I've seen him twice in concert, and I know all the words and can rap it like a champ. It was my go-to song during my final board interview for EO (Entrepreneurs Organization)—where I busted out the lyrics like I owned it! I always thought I just liked that song because it made me happy to sing it, and I was proud that I could remember all the lyrics. But upon deeper reflection, I realized something new: the lyrics are the exact opposite of feeling left out and frustrated. The whole song is about "I have arrived, and the party can begin!"

Hearing that song puts a smile on my face every time. I just want to get up and dance. So within the first thirty seconds of hearing this music—bam!—I'm down an entirely different neural pathway that is very different from "Jar of Hearts." I'm feeling blessed, I'm feeling included, I'm feeling exuberant about life, and I've got a whole crowd around to support me. And so, yes, I went right to my sound system and turned up the bass and danced around my living room like when I saw Bruno at BottleRock. There's no space for feeling anything but elated around this song.

Identifying the playlist that is holding you back can be difficult. A good coach can help you crystallize it. And they can ask the right questions to help you home in on what the exact title is that would best shift that old neural pathway. It's different for everyone. Most recently, Barbara, an executive I worked with, realized she had a pattern of constantly evaluating people and experiences as good or bad. Through our conversation, she realized that she makes the same judgments about everything she does, even how she looks in the mirror. We called her old playlist "I'm Not Pretty Enough," and with that as a backdrop, she could see how she was constantly evaluating her own worth, where she was or wasn't enough, and the same for everyone else in her life. The songs on her old playlist included "I Love Me" from Demi Lovato. It's a song about superficial beauty standards imposed from outside. It's about hiding within yourself or behind a mask and comparing yourself to everyone around you.

Once you see your wound and how that playlist ties into it, all you want to do is fix it, and Barbara was no different.

"What should be the new playlist?" she asked.

I offered a new idea, thinking it might be the antidote: "How about 'I'm Fabulous'?"

Nope. That felt too arrogant to wrap her arms around. If the playlist doesn't resonate, it's going to be hard to shift away from the old one. So then I asked her to connect to a memory she had as a child, when this messaging of not being attractive enough was particularly activated.

"My mom was constantly critiquing what I wore and how I looked," she said. "I learned early on that you have to keep yourself looking good if you want to get ahead in this world."

"So it's served you in some way as a motivation tool?" I asked.

"Yes, that's right, and I still believe that," she said. "You are more likely to get a job, promotion, etcetera, if you look attractive."

You can see how committed she was to this belief, to this playlist. I asked her to think about a particularly distressing memory where she felt she was not enough, to put herself back in her little girl shoes for a moment and reconnect to that experience. Then I asked to her to imagine that she is the parent of that little girl.

"What do you want to say to that little one who comes to you and says, 'Mommy, I'm worried I'm not pretty enough'? What do you want her to believe instead? How would you comfort her?"

"I'd say, 'You are uniquely beautiful!'" There were tears in her eyes.

"Then that's your new playlist," I said. "Let's fill it with songs that represent that message to you."

As an anchoring song, we picked Bruno Mars's "Just the Way You Are" and added some fun with Meghan Trainor's "Me Too." Her assignment was to fill out the rest of the playlist and listen to the songs every time she works out or makes dinner and to dance around if she wants to—but recognizing that the messages of these songs are reflective of how she needs to start treating herself. The more she loves herself and stops judging herself, the less she will judge others. Her work and personal relationships immediately began to improve dramatically.

Not everyone has a coach or has the opportunity to work with a coach, so I'd like to give you some resources to help you do this for yourself. Only you can come up with the new playlist that's going to work for you. But here's how you kickstart the process in a nutshell.

When you are clear on the old playlist title but not sure about the new one, see if you can access a memory from your childhood where you feel that old title got activated. It doesn't have to be the first time (although that's helpful), just one where you still might have a little emotional charge about it when you think about it. Now, imagine yourself as the parent of that little one, and he or she comes to you and says the statement of the old playlist to you. What would you want to say back to comfort him or her? What does she or he need to hear? What would best help that child to believe something about himself or herself that would help him or her in life? That message is the start of your new playlist.

We are not trying to blame your parents for not saying the right thing to you. Your parents didn't necessarily know what you needed to hear, and they may not have realized the significance you would place on their messaging. Your parents didn't say the thing you needed to hear, but you can do it now. And the more you do it, the more you'll start to believe it and integrate it, freeing yourself from the shackles that old message placed on you. You can reach your highest potential by changing your playlist and thus resetting your reactions.

The bottom line is that music can be a powerful tool to rewire your brain patterns. If researchers can use music to manipulate our levels of productivity, bodily functions such as heart rate, and emotional states such as anxiety, why not take that power into your own hands? Why not harness this tool to improve your leadership by interrupting your wound and workplace triggers? As much as the trigger feels real in the moment, it is just another scratch in the neural pathway that was grooved long ago. We can use the power of music to bring this pattern to consciousness, so that we can intentionally shift it to something far more productive. Then we can use the power of music to help us groove a new neural pathway, one that is far more enlightened and can help us show up as the mature, adult leader; not the leader ravaged by childhood wounds.

3

Free Bird

David,[1] a CEO in his early forties, is a visionary thinker. He built a successful event management company that supported major sports awards, company conventions, and media company launches. His quick wit and great communication skills enabled him to envision an exciting and transformative event space, with unique touches and surprises that would "wow" guests. His creative genius was his superpower. However, handling the nuts and bolts of running a team and a business was his liability. He frequently changed direction and changed his mind on how he wanted things to look. This would create shock waves throughout his organization, causing people to scramble and shift course. While his team appreciated the desire to make the best possible experience for a client, he seemed to go way overboard and wasted a lot of resources pursuing perfection.

David's blind spot was thinking he could run the company the same way with eighty employees as he had with ten—he just would not accept that they couldn't pivot so quickly anymore.

"He has no idea of the ramifications of his whims," one employee told me. "We are frustrated as hell, and it's hard to keep staff, because they work so hard on one design, only to have it thrown out at the last minute and work longer hours to satisfy the latest iteration."

When confronted with this, David explained, "That's the creative process. We aren't going to stay locked into one design if, as it's going up, I see there are better ways to meet the client's goals. That's what makes our company brilliant." Logically, David needed to find a balance between putting on the most amazing event possible and cost-effectively producing the event while keeping his team engaged along the way.

But there was something more at play, and it was sitting in the deeper layers of David's behavior set long ago. We slowly uncovered it by exploring David's biggest triggers. I started by asking, "What can drive you crazy when working with others? What's your biggest pet peeve?" As he listed what could annoy him about collaborating with other people, I started to see themes in the way he approached his work. It helped to hear specific examples to the questions: "When was the last time you were triggered at work, and what happened? Why do you think you were triggered?"

"I need freedom, and I hate to be told what to do," he shared.

I asked him, "And how does that show up as a trigger?"

"When people say, 'You can't do that,' it kind of makes me crazy. And I want to prove to them that I *can* do it."

"How does that show up with your team?" I asked.

"When I get a great idea and I'm excited and I bring it to my team, they want to throw cold water on it. They get so rigid it's like pulling teeth. And I'm the CEO! They should just execute!"

"Hmm," I said. "So they don't like being just told what to do and execute? Sounds familiar."

"Yeah. . . . I see what you mean." Light bulbs went off for him, but he was still defending himself. He said, "But I'm the CEO, and that's what I hired them for. *I'm* the creative genius."

"That's an interesting assumption," I said. "Imagine you come to work for you. How would it feel to have a boss like you?"

"If I had the creative genius, probably stifling," he admitted.

"And so your team doesn't have any creative genius?"

"No, no. I hired some of the best. They may not have my eye, but compared to what's out there, I appreciate their vision to incorporate my ideas and make it come alive."

"And so, given that they do have talent, what do you think it's like to work for you? Could this be related to your talent retention problem?"

He stared at me with his mouth open as more light bulbs started to click on.

Here's a little secret in leadership development: Your talent retention problem is *always* an issue of your leadership. As much as leaders like to fight it, it's not your "entitled employees"; it's you. Your job is to select and retain the best talent possible. If you aren't doing that, there is something to explore in your leadership style.

So let's look deeper at how this kind of programming got started for David. I asked him about the earliest triggering event he could recall as a child. I told him that it should be one which, thinking back on it, still might have an emotional charge or distress around it. He said it used to drive him crazy that his mother was a "borderline narcissist." His distress, he said, was always all about her; his dad was the sweetest, kindest man, and he just kept trying to please her.

"She never took responsibility for anything that went wrong. She would just find things to complain and worry about. I would watch my

Dad bend over backwards to make her happy, and she was never satisfied. He took care of everything while she barely lifted a finger—and still she complained."

"How did her complaining and your dad's pleasing behavior affect you?" I asked.

"I just wanted to get the hell out of there, because the dynamic was infuriating. But, also, she would complain that my brother and I didn't do our chores to her liking, which made it even worse."

"And so how did you cope with that?"

"I just found things to take my mind off of it and escape, so to speak. I'd organize events for the neighborhood gang, and, as a teenager, I'd plan outlandish events for my friends. I think that is where my love for event planning began. I guess I realize now that I felt very confined by my mother and her mindset. I just wanted to be free of it all. I wanted to be free to make my own decisions, free to do it my way, not her way, which felt obnoxiously anal to me. I felt trapped by her constant nitpicking and micromanagement."

So, you can see, the internal playlist on repeat for David is "I Am Trapped." Internally, the message is *I felt trapped by my mother; no way, no how am I going to let that happen again.* So, running from this monster shows up as a need to constantly iterate. David needed to prove to himself that the monster he was running from hadn't caught up with him. The fear of being constrained is akin to claustrophobia: If you don't have an escape hatch, you feel as though you could be stuck in this situation forever.

What David realized is that his need for freedom, that need to not be constrained, was still running him in unproductive ways. He didn't want to be constrained by initial plans and didn't think twice about changing up the design for an event, no matter the cost. He essentially overvalued his need for choice and undervalued the cost of making those changes—to the detriment of others.

"Wow," he said. "I guess, in some ways, my team might see me as a narcissist, too. All this time, I've been justifying my behavior under the umbrella of 'creative genius' without taking a look at the cost of that to others."

Choosing a playlist is personal. Only you know what songs will resonate with you and accurately capture your emotional inner world. That said, if I had to choose one for David, I would suggest that his old playlist incorporated songs like "Free Bird" by Lynyrd Skynyrd. That iconic song clearly expresses the need to be free. If things become too constraining, the narrator suggests, escape to the next thing. David never wanted to be locked into one design, because then he might be stuck with it; that's the feeling he is running from. So even when the design didn't really need to be tweaked, when it was just as good as the second, third, and fourth iterations, David's playlist led him to continually tinker to feel that freedom of expression.

Like any leadership trait, David's sense of claustrophobia, combined with his creativity, is not all good or all bad. Leaders repeating this playlist have the gifts of vision and of communicating inspiring outcomes. People appreciate their ability to think creatively and outside the box, and to communicate in clear terms what success will look like. Always finding a way to make something even better, this wounded leader revises a project again and again until it matches the vision they intend.

But the constant revision can leave their team feeling depleted and disengaged when their hard work gets thrown out the window for each successive version. Fearing getting stuck with a decision they can't change, this playlist may cause the leader to hesitate to embrace a single course of action. They are often blind to the vast corporate resources that are wasted when they—and so their team—struggle with indecision. "We're still waiting for the green light" becomes the norm, and despite loving innovation and making things better and better, this leader ends up stalling progress and profitability in the effort to avoid being trapped.

This type of leader may also fear taking on debt to infuse the company with necessary capital to grow, feeling that the debt would weigh heavily or become a prison that they'll be trapped in. They may also feel unwilling to take on a board of directors through private-equity investment, which can help guide the company. The wounded leader fears that the board may tell them what to do and that they will lose autonomy. In either case, the organization's growth is stunted by the leader's fear driving their behavior.

Becoming aware of the corporate resources (time and money) that are wasted through indecision is an important path of growth. So is the ability to accept guidance without feeling stifled. An enlightened leader can balance vision with execution to bring the most creative and disruptive ideas to the market effectively and without alienating the team, the board, or the customers.

When I work with leaders of this type, I usually ask *why* they want to scale their business and whether they are conscious of what will need to shift in their leadership to make that happen. If they feel constrained by repeatable processes and greater structure, I may even go so far as to suggest that they sell the company to someone else and go start a new one. That gift of unrestrained creativity can be harnessed in creating a new venture, but it's much less effective in growing a functional organization.

As your company scales from forty to sixty to one hundred people, your unrestrained creativity has costs. The organization just can't handle the whiplash of creative whims; you have to deliver consistently for the client. Think of it like a speed boat versus a ship. When your boat is small, you are able to shift course and feel the thrill of the wind and waves. As you add more people to your business, you need a bigger boat.

When you get to the size of a large yacht or a barge, you can't make those sudden moves like you used to, and you feel those thrilling waves much less. You must know your course (your secret sauce) and must follow it consistently—that is, leverage the heck out of it. I'm not saying you can't innovate, but you need to be much more intentional about when innovation is warranted and when to follow the chart. You also need to provide enough support to the organization to handle that pivot. David, like other entrepreneurs, wanted to feel the freedom of the speed boat, but he had a large yacht on his hands. If he didn't manage that appropriately, he would be unable to keep people on his boat, and he may even capsize. Like other leaders of his type, the reason he was stuck operating his business like a speed boat has its roots in his childhood wounds.

The new playlist had to be something compelling to David. "I'd really like to build a company where we create something incredible together and I stop dictating to them the way my mom did to me." David realized that to truly feel free, he needed to feel that others had his back—that their concerns with implementation weren't an attempt to limit him. We came up with the song "Freedom! '90" from George Michael. The obvious key lyric is the battle cry of "Freedom!," but there is also a strong theme of support and confidence. The song's story starts with indecision and even a sense of entanglement; the narrator had accepted his early fate. But then he embraces his need for change and turns it into huge success. Along the way, he supports his partners and joins with them to grow. He promises not to let them down, not to give them up. He breaks out of his confinement by embracing his strengths without letting them trap him.

This is David to a T, describing his journey from wounded to enlightened leader. David needed to feel dependability and to be dependable himself. He realized he was running from feeling constrained, his old trigger. Instead, he got connected to something more meaningful; something that was more dependable for him: creating an environment where the best creative talent would thrive and produce the most unique events in the country. It didn't need to be all about him (which was ironically the same issue he had with his mom).

Ultimately, David signed on to manage his automatic response: Instead of insisting on driving the yacht like a speed boat, he now understood the responsibility of managing a larger vessel. He did this by connecting to what was possible for the company and his customers and by making the vision far more compelling than the fear of constraint. In this way, he was running toward something rather than away from something.

Some leaders like David decide they don't want this responsibility and become serial entrepreneurs, learning to hand a project off when the company gets too big for them to drive their speed boat. I don't make a value judgment on either strategy; they're both valid ways of understanding your old playlist and deciding how to change it for a better experience. The key is that understanding: If you are simply dancing to your old tunes, that playlist is running you. The real freedom that you seek can come only from changing your songs to what you want to hear.

COMPARING PLAYLISTS

Although we focus on a single song each for the wounded and enlightened versions of our example leaders, let's keep in mind that those songs are part of larger playlists. I think it's important to have one signature, or anchor, song for the old and new playlist. Mine was "Jar of Hearts" for the old and "24K Magic" for the new. Those were the songs that most perfectly captured how I used to feel and how I wanted to feel.

We need to identify our old playlist because remembering that song can help you identify when you are in the old emotional pattern or frequency. For the old playlist, that one song may be enough for you to catch yourself early on when your thinking is leading you to the highway to hell. One client I worked with used Adele's song "Hello" as the reminder of her old playlist about being left out. Then, when she would catch herself starting to perceive a certain situation as being left out, she would say, "Oh, there's Adele again!" and she would literally laugh at herself. It would bring some humor and levity, and allow her to shift from replaying her wound over and over to getting onto the new playlist of "I Am Valuable," because that's how she really wanted to feel.

The brain likes variety, so when you are creating a new playlist and a new neural pathway, having several songs helps you to maintain the emotional frequency you would prefer to continue to emanate. With the new playlist, I highly recommend that you add as many songs as you like that create the preferred emotional state. At the end of each chapter, I include the anchor song for our heroes' wounded state and their healed state that allow them to achieve enlightened leadership. Your own playlists will be unique to you—what you feel, what you need, and how you'll grow. Feel free to leverage these to inspire your own playlist based on your own preferred genre (country, rap, rock, etc.).

DAVID'S OLD PLAYLIST: "I AM TRAPPED"

Anchor Song: "Free Bird" by Lynyrd Skynyrd

SUPERPOWERS

- Creativity
- Vision
- Innovation

- Being prolific
- Originality

LIABILITIES

- Flighty behavior
- Indecision
- A lack of commitment
- Poor execution
- Constant brainstorming or iterating

DAVID'S NEW PLAYLIST: "I CAN DEPEND ON YOU"

Anchor Song: "Freedom! '90" by George Michael

For the full list of songs in David's playlist, both old and new, and for a document that can provide inspiration to create your own, visit www.theleadersplaylistbook.com or scan the QR code below.

If you would like a head start on identifying your wound—and its corresponding superpower—take the Enlightened Leadership assessment to discover your path to enlightened leadership. This is a simple quiz designed to point in the direction of your wound, not to be a definitive answer to it (which would be fairly unlikely in a seven-question quiz). As you read your results, look to see what resonates and what doesn't, and then compare with the other wounds we have identified. We welcome your feedback and suggestions to continue to level up the quality of the results. You can find the quiz at www.susandrumm.com or by scanning the QR code below.

4

Natural

In your search for enlightened leadership, it's important to note that simply leveraging your strengths and expecting them to carry you through a crisis could come back to bite you. Leadership requires balance; you must know both your strengths and your weaknesses. The overuse of a leadership strength without balance opens you up to blind spots and potential areas of failure. The following example illustrates this well.

Tom was the CEO of a fast-growing tech company. He is an incredibly charismatic, take-charge kind of guy. When he speaks, people listen. He started his company to fill a product gap, confident that he'd soon dominate the market. Tom loved being the underdog, and his tenacity to be a disrupter in the marketplace was the fuel that kept him working late hours. This bravado enabled him to hire some heavy hitters in the industry, and he assembled quite a talented executive team. As the company grew and the market feedback came back very strong, Tom only grew more emboldened. As they prepared for market launch, he hired key employees away from a competitor. The competitor did not take kindly to that and slapped Tom's fledging business with a significant lawsuit.

Tom's confidence, his signature leadership strength, continued even in the initial stages of the lawsuit. Then some potentially damaging evidence came to light. Tom realized he had overreached. His confidence—which had grown to the point of arrogance—came back to bite him. With the company's plans to launch on hold for at least six months, funding was running low. The leadership team had to come to grips with possibly laying off half of their workforce.

Before this setback, Tom was true to his nature: He didn't want to get 360 data on himself or to receive coaching. He hired my firm to work with his leadership team on issues they were having, but he wasn't open to looking deeper into himself. Underneath this reticence was an attempt to avoid feeling vulnerable. Tom used his bravado to cover for his perceived weakness—perceived by himself, not his colleagues. This self-doubt may have been subconscious, and it was certainly hidden from others. He had begun with a useful shell of confidence, but it had morphed into arrogance. Tom's wound showed up in the workplace the same way every leader's wounds show up. If you don't do the healing work to create a new playlist, you'll eventually play the wounded one for everyone around you.

Had Tom initially embraced the development work along with his staff, I firmly believe the lawsuit could have been averted. Obviously, we can't see our own blind spots; that's why they are called blind spots. Thorough 360-degree feedback can help us to recognize what others see in our professional persona.

As I assessed the rest of Tom's team, it was clear that Tom's problem was central. Despite addressing their own areas needing improvement, the team as a whole could never succeed without its leader also looking at himself. It's not that he was a bad leader. His staff loved him and his "we-are-going-to-win" gusto. But they did harbor reservations that they were overlooking things. They all thought they should be more cautious in their strategy and should explore potential downfalls. None of them ever thought they could take Tom aside and say, "Hey, what if our competitor files a lawsuit against us after we steal their people?" Because of his unflinching confidence, some of them believed that Tom would always win a fight, and the others didn't believe he'd listen to their concerns.

After Tom realized he had misjudged the impact a lawsuit would have on his ability to launch, he finally agreed to undertake the exercise of looking deeper into his own blind spot. He found the courage to take in and analyze his wound. It was crystal clear in his report. Having the opportunity to do some deeper work and understand the play-list behind Tom's behavior saved Tom—and his team—from further mistakes and opened him up to regularly asking his team for their perspectives. Learning about his underlying wound and the behaviors that resulted from it allowed Tom to stop using only the default position of his leadership. He could now choose when to employ his confidence and when to employ some other tool, like analyzing the downside risk. The ability to balance and blend is crucial.

Leaders like Tom, who verge on being overconfident, often have experienced or witnessed emotional or physical abuse. Their arrogance springs directly from the desire to protect themselves and the people around them. In Tom's case, it was a domineering father who physically and emotionally abused his mother. This was compounded by the fact that they lived in a dangerous neighborhood. Growing up in a dangerous environment tends to produce a fear response—a response that inspires leaders like Tom to fight to survive.

This type of leader is keenly aware of what could happen if they don't fight back. Any circumstance of conflict as an adult triggers that hardwiring, creating an outsized response of anger or aggression. Often we see anger flare up in the workplace, which can be experienced by other team members as bullying. At its extreme, it could lead to harassment charges (sexual, gender, etc.), but it can also create a "yes man" workforce that seeks to comply with the bully. On the less extreme side of these behaviors is a general arrogance like Tom's that is used as a shield. This leader believes—perhaps subconsciously—that if they project themselves as larger than life, they are less likely to be attacked. As we saw with Tom's team, the effect of this attitude is that others in the organization are less likely to challenge the leader or suggest a different option, because they sense that the leader is not open to their ideas or having a change of mind. Without the team members who are closest to the situation giving their honest opinions, the leader is missing information when making critical decisions—and is more susceptible to making bad decisions that are costly to the organization.

This type of leader also tends to have a deep understanding of strength in numbers. Like forming a gang to fight another gang, this leader forms a close-knit group of supporters with their leadership team. This mentality relies on the presupposition that there are "good" guys and "bad" guys. By this very construct, "we" have to be the good guys and need to identify someone else as the "bad guy" to prove our righteousness and our strength. Thus, we will provoke our perceived enemy and draw ourselves into a battle so that we can prove our strength to overcome.

The playlist title running Tom could be called "I Am Not Safe." With his fear of attack operating in the background, Tom was constantly vigilant, looking for potential threats in the environment. Subconsciously hating the fact that he lived in a world where he doesn't feel safe, Tom did everything he could think of to create safety. This type of leader runs from their fear by being larger than life, fiercer than anyone. They beat their chest like a silverback gorilla. Even more, they take risks to prove themselves, poking the sleeping dragon (whatever that may be) so that they can show their courage to face it. Until they heal this pattern of behavior, they are going to attract circumstances that require them to fight, and some battles they will not win.

If we had to boil it down to a representative song, the "I Am Not Safe" playlist might begin with "Natural" by Imagine Dragons. The narrator is boastful and aggressive. The song tells the story of someone broken by their circumstances who must employ cutthroat tactics to survive. It describes a world without peace—cold and dark and dangerous. This is how leaders with this playlist title often see the world; it's the world they were taught to see when they were young. And, much like the song's narrator, Tom would rather be the hunter than the prey. He was always on the attack, always expecting confrontation.

Like any other behavior, there is a blessing and a curse to (over) confidence like Tom's. The blessing is that it takes an incredible drive to accomplish big goals, and this leader often refuses to let anything stand in their way. This pattern is effective in galvanizing others to rally behind a cause, to take action, and push themselves harder than they might otherwise have done. The team led by this type of leader can accomplish great feats of heroism. Leading comes easily to businesspeople like Tom, and many employees feel comfortable letting them take charge.

However, the curse is also a part of the equation. These teams often become embroiled in fights they cannot win. If they are overly arrogant, relying on this single strength, they may experience burnout and depletion from all the fighting. In the latter case, I've often seen health challenges creep up for the leader and those fighting the battle with them; they often fail to acknowledge that they need to rest, recover, and restore. I've even heard leaders of this type brag about how little sleep they need, but then they face back or heart issues from overextending themselves.

So, what is the antidote to feeling unsafe? Would you be shocked to hear the phrase "Love thy neighbor"? I'm not suggesting you have to love your competition, but I am suggesting that you turn your attention from another company being your target to serving your customer more effectively and holistically. That's an important mind shift and has more sustainability as a cause for you and your team (and it's healthier).

In Tom's case, he finally embraced the process of working on himself and learning about his wounds and how they affect his behavior. He learned that his pattern was to subconsciously look for—or even create—fights, so he could prove his strength. To help him discover this, we first did a series of interviews to get feedback on his team—a 360-degree assessment. Receiving that feedback, coupled with recognizing the misjudgment that led to the lawsuit, allowed Tom to realize how arrogant he had been in his leadership.

We then took a deeper look at why he came across as arrogant. What did he feel he needed to project such certainty and confidence about? Tom shared his belief that it was important to show strength in order to be successful. I asked where that belief came from, and that's when he suggested it came from his rough childhood.

Then I asked, "Can you share a memory of when you felt threatened but you fought back and felt victorious?"

He shared a memory of a kid coming at him with a baseball bat. Tom stood up to the kid and avoided violence. That kid later became one of his best friends.

To move beyond posturing against shadows, it helps to expand your gang or team. Rather than searching for battles close to home, find a bigger purpose. You might want your company to combat climate change or to improve the lives of the local community members. Instead of looking for something to fight against, you can find something worth fighting for.

We called Tom's new playlist "I Feel Safe," and our first song on the list was "A Million Dreams" by Pink. This song is optimistic and powerful, and it conveys strong confidence without turning to arrogance. It's about creating a vision, but not alone—the narrator wants to bring the listener along to a new world. This is a great model for a leader who wants to bring their team—and their entire organization—along with them. In the song, they work together to make something better.

Form a purpose beyond just winning over your competitor. With this attitude, you can rally the team around how your product or service will enrich the lives of others, save the planet, protect precious resources. When you make that larger vision your battle cry, you'll be surprised at how many of your team and community members—maybe even those competitors—will join your cause.

When you heal your wound, you become an enlightened leader. Rather than projecting arrogance or always looking for a fight, you can now leverage your confidence. Use your connection to a meaningful mission to blast through obstacles and setbacks. Rather than fighting every imagined dragon, you can create a positive difference in the world, making a million dreams come true.

 COMPARING PLAYLISTS

TOM'S OLD PLAYLIST: "I DON'T FEEL SAFE"

Anchor Song: "Natural" by Imagine Dragons

SUPERPOWERS

- Confidence

- Tackling big challenges
- Leadership that provides assurance to others

LIABILITIES

- Looking for a fight
- Arrogance
- Bravado
- Defensiveness
- Extreme risk taking
- Or its opposite—being extremely conservative

TOM'S NEW PLAYLIST: "I FEEL SAFE"

Anchor Song: "A Million Dreams" by Pink

For the full list of songs in Tom's playlist, both old and new, and for a document that can provide inspiration to create your own, visit www.theleadersplaylistbook.com or scan the QR code below.

5

Survivor

Sahar was a phenomenal workhorse. A child of immigrant parents, she put herself through college by working two jobs while also raising a child (from an unplanned pregnancy). This work ethic enabled her to rise up through the ranks of a digital payment company to the role of president of a key division, reporting to the CEO.

Despite all of this success, Sahar still had a chip on her shoulder. Deep down, she felt inferior to her peers, who had gone to fancier, Ivy League schools and had MBAs. They generally came from more privileged backgrounds than she did. Because she viewed herself that way, she was hypervigilant for veiled or imagined insults. She seemed to be constantly seeking evidence to confirm that others believed she was less than they were. If someone tried to suggest that the way she was running her division wasn't working, she fiercely defended her turf. She protected her people like a lioness over her cubs and wanted to make sure any request for them to collaborate with others in some way came through her first. It was very clear to her colleagues that she had an inner circle and an outer circle. If you were in the inner circle, she trusted you with her life, but if you were in the outer circle, you were perceived as a potential threat.

While the CEO loved her performance within her division, her uncollaborative style with the other division presidents was causing a lot of strife in the management committee, and he was starting to tire of being a mediator. Coaching was deemed a good investment, so Sahar came to me.

You can imagine that going into a coaching engagement this way is challenging for the coach. There usually isn't much engagement from the coachee at first. These are some of the toughest assignments, and the only way through is to identify a pain point that the client is having, and start the coaching there to see what opens up for them.

Naturally, Sahar wanted help getting *others* to change, rather than seeking her own growth. But that's not what coaching is about. You can't get others to change through coaching; you can only learn to change yourself and your reaction to those others. Through the work we did together, Sahar was able to weave in the wounds of her past and understand how they were coloring her perspective now.

"I've always had to fight for everything," she said. "I had to fight to go to college, had to fight off the girl gang at school. I even had to fight off my attacker, but I wasn't successful." It was then that she opened up about being raped by her uncle. Her family didn't believe her and an inner rage grew inside her. It's no surprise at all that she learned to survive by making a clear delineation between who she could trust and who she couldn't. It was better, she reasoned, to come out with a fierce disposition and not be taken advantage of than to let others take from her. Obviously, these are pretty traumatic wounds. As most coaches would do, I encouraged her to work with a therapist who specializes in sexual abuse.

Sahar learned at an early age that in order to survive, she needed to toughen up and come out swinging. And so to protect herself, she developed a form of hypervigilance for where and when the next attack might come. Not only was she wary of it; she *expected* it. Better to be prepared than to be caught off guard.

Certainly, Sahar had plenty of experience in her life where she was treated unfairly, and given that was also a central theme in my own playlist, I could connect deeply with the fear that was running her. Sahar developed a heightened sensitivity to threat, and perceived threats where there may be none.

The people around you always read your signals. If you are sending out an emotional signal of "I've got to defend myself and my people," then it's clear to others that you live in constant fear of impending threats. Leaders like this are prone to a defensive posture (or even offensive posture) because the fear of being taken advantage of is running them. You will see it show up in behaviors like Sahar's: aggressively defending her team, fighting for a bigger salary in an unproductive way, and blaming others for her responses. Colleagues who work with these types of leader feel the frustration of being misinterpreted, shy away from giving real feedback, and ultimately ostracize them. This creates a self-fulling prophecy: The "unfairly treated" leader is treated differently, and that makes leaders like Sahar feel their responses are justified.

This sort of protective leader has the gift of strength, and with fierce and inspiring vigilance, they protect what is most valuable to them. Their team often feels like the leader has their back. They cherish the loyalty and trust the leader shows them, and exhibit those traits in return. This leader's courage to stand up to others who try to exploit their people can be impressive and inspiring.

Similar to Tom, Sahar was always on the alert for an incoming attack. But instead of exhibiting arrogance, Sahar focused on fiercely protecting herself and her inner circle. The title of Sahar's initial playlist could be "I Am Treated Unfairly." A central song on this playlist would be "Survivor" by Destiny's Child. The song is obviously about survival, but it approaches the idea from a posture of aggressive defense. The narrator has removed some abusive or unsupportive person from their life, and they are better off for it. They not only fend off any attack, but they are stronger, richer, harder, and wiser afterward. They survive. But they survive by working harder, never giving up, and constantly defending themselves. That takes a lot of energy. The truth is that Sahar wanted to thrive, not just survive. Frankly, as she told me during more retrospective moments, she was exhausted from having to defend herself 24/7.

The behaviors related to this playlist include defensiveness, resentment, and seeing things through the lens of being constantly attacked. Rather than focusing on what is going well and being grateful for opportunities, this leader's awareness is focused on how they aren't getting their fair share. This particularly shows up during year-end compensation time, where the person is almost never happy with their comp or raise and is always complaining, because, of course, if they don't fight, they will be taken advantage of. And yet, over time, their boss may get so frustrated that they end up finding a reason to let them go. This further inflicts a wound in the leader, more evidence that they were treated unfairly. Turnover like this is costly in any scenario—and I've had leaders say "They were competent. If only they were easier to work with, we could have had a great relationship." Now, they have to search for a replacement due to this type of behavior.

Another manifestation of extreme overprotectiveness with one's own team and difficulty collaborating with other parts of the organization is that key information exchange between departments is limited and guarded, slowing innovation and timely response to external challenges.

Interestingly, sometimes an opposite behavior crops up with this playlist title running in the background. This person wants to trust, wants to believe that they will get what they deserve, and so naively only takes in data that supports this wishful thinking. It's an extreme example of "running from" behavior. This leader wants so much not to be treated unfairly that they refuse to see any data that might suggest that they are. Only after something completely blows up in their face (a project, a marketing campaign, a lawsuit) do they realize how naive they have been.

If you are being run by this playlist, you may have developed a heightened sensitivity to potential threats, and you may read threats where there are none. Alternatively, you may tend toward the other extreme, where you put blinders on to potential threats, exposing yourself to being taken advantage of, and thereby creating the conditions that drive the need to rise up to defend yourself. Your work is to notice where you are being hypervigilant for evidence that confirms others believe you are less than they are and to focus your attention on all the blessings you have received.

To change the pattern would enable Sahar to have a more accurate perception and understanding of her colleagues' behaviors. Together, we applied the same process of understanding the current playlist that was running her and creating a new, more empowering playlist. She also had to let go of the inferiority complex and learn to love herself even more for all the obstacles she had to overcome to get to her position.

With Sahar, we spent a good deal of time focused on how the old behavior was draining her mentally and physically. She felt exhausted, frustrated, and worn out from the constant battling. This was her bellyful—when she reached her limit with the status quo. This is the first and most important step toward true change. She realized that something needed to change or she might have a nervous breakdown. And because she now understood that the only way to experience change was to change herself, she was onboard to get this playlist off the airwaves and create a new one.

And to find that new one, we focused on the emotional state she really wanted to feel. I asked her, "Instead of feeling exhausted, frustrated, and worn out, what would you really like to be feeling?" She recalled a moment she recently had on a beach vacation where she got an unexpected upgrade to a corner suite with a balcony overlooking the ocean. She was overjoyed in the moment and felt such gratitude and peace. "I want to feel that way again!" she exclaimed. We created her new playlist together to reconnect with that feeling.

We called Sahar's new playlist "I Am Blessed." She chose songs about gratitude and peace. A good example is "There's Nothing Holdin' Me Back" by Shawn Mendes. It's a love song, but beyond the relationship aspect it's about a person who embraces their own power. With nothing holding them back, they know that everything will be alright. They feel no fear and can take on any challenge they come across. But this song brought more than the lyrics to heal Sahar's wounds. It created a beautiful emotional state in Sahar when she heard it. It brought her right back to that feeling of being blessed and having a sense of peace that she experienced on that beach vacation.

Between the work she did with her therapist and her coach, Sahar began to heal herself. She widened her inner circle to include the entire company and projected her outer circle to be the company's biggest rival. She got deeply connected to why she wanted the company to win, not just herself to win. Instead of protecting herself, she used that fierce energy to protect the company, and in the process blasted away the walls that were keeping her from forming stronger relationships internally.

As one colleague put it, "I can't tell you what a relief it is to feel like we are working on the same side, versus feeling like I was the enemy. I used to dread interactions with her, and now I'm learning so much more than I ever dreamed from Sahar." And Sahar noticed in herself a lightness in her presence that wasn't there before. "I feel so much happier," she shared. "It's like I finally feel free to let some of the armor down that I used to protect myself. I'm not that little girl anymore. I've got this."

COMPARING PLAYLISTS

SAHAR'S OLD PLAYLIST: "I'M TREATED UNFAIRLY"

Anchor Song: "Survivor" by Destiny's Child

SUPERPOWERS

- Being a protector
- Courage
- Inspiration

LIABILITIES

- Defensiveness
- Blaming others
- Fierceness
- Overprotectiveness
- Or its opposite—naivety

SAHAR'S NEW PLAYLIST: "I AM BLESSED"

Anchor Song: "There's Nothing Holdin' Me Back" by Shawn Mendes

For the full list of songs in Sahar's playlist, both old and new, and for a document that can provide inspiration to create your own, visit www.theleadersplaylistbook.com or scan the QR code below.

6

Winning

Those who are most in need of creating a new playlist are those in power today: current CEOs and senior executives. They have the ability to make rapid transformation before the next generation takes the helm. I'm talking about small and large business leaders alike; I've seen each use their success in business to avoid doing the real work that true leadership requires.

For instance, take Michael, a CEO of a successful therapeutic drug company with about four hundred employees in his early fifties. He's proud of the fact that he works harder than anyone else, and says how much he loves his work. However, when you dig beneath the surface, the reason he "loves" his work is that it provides a safe refuge from his anxiety. He feels he can control his work, especially given that he *is* in control, as the CEO of his company. He feels good when he feels productive, crossing things off the list, but then his life becomes one cycle of adding things to the list and crossing them off. However, he is never really present to the consequences of this obsession with productivity and control. The workaholic whose self-worth is tied up with their business success is most at risk, because all of that can be wiped out with the next wave of disruption.

Michael is also not present to the cost of this drive on his personal and work relationships. At home, his kids barely know him and are creating their own wounds and stories around Daddy not caring about their lives. At work, his employees have learned to be very efficient with their meeting time with him, but they don't trust him enough to create the kind of loyalty required to retain talent when things get tough. They've learned that the "just get it done" attitude is rewarded, but coming up with new, out of the box ideas that may fail is too risky to push for with Michael. Without innovation, Michael has set his team up for failure in the wave of disruption that is affecting every industry.

It will be a hard day for Michael when he suffers a failure he didn't expect. He may get hit with a major life event, such as his wife filing for divorce, a heart attack from not exercising enough, or a more nimble competitor reaching the market faster. A leader like Michael may need a wake-up call before he begins the hard work of looking at how his wounds are driving his behavior.

When we eventually did dig deeper, we found that Michael learned early on that he felt as though his parents only loved him when he got As. "If I don't succeed, they don't love me," he said. So he's been driven to perform ever since, tying his own self-worth to the success he has in business. He became the stereotypical successful workaholic, whose underlying fear of failure drives them to inadvertently destroy their marriage, scar their children, and lose friendships because they're always too busy. The irony is that, in his pursuit to win, he's losing the love in his current relationships with the people who are most important to him.

We called Michael's initial playlist "I Must Succeed to Be Loved." He can never win enough or be successful enough to fill the hole that this wound created, although he is damn sure he is going to try. And he'll have all the justifications for why his behavior is warranted.

Michael chose as an anchor song "Winning" by Santana to capture how he lived his life and was obsessed with success. As the singer keeps obsessively chanting "I'm winning! I'm winning!" Michael started to see how his laser-focused obsession on being successful was actually robbing his joy. In the song, the artist refuses to lose, and that's how Michael's workaholism manifests itself. He cannot lose, so he cannot let anything distract himself (even the love of his family) from accomplishing his goals.

If you are repeating this playlist, you have the gift of tireless dedication to achieving outcomes that matter. You are laser focused on the organization's goals, and you disregard extraneous activities to zero in on what is most important to creating the result you want. People value your reliability in delivering successful outcomes, and they know that if anyone is going to get it done, it's you.

With this playlist on in the background, you may get a high from being productive. However, you may get trapped in the cycle of adding things to the list and crossing them off without really being present to the consequences of being too focused on simply accomplishing tasks. If you aren't constantly ticking off boxes, it can feel like you are wasting time. You lose yourself within the safe refuge of work to keep anxiety at bay. The risk is that your relationships, both work and personal, could suffer.

For this type of leader, winning is everything and the only thing that matters. Their entire sense of self is wrapped up in their success, as is their self-perceived value. To get to that success, they may cut corners; they may even endanger their own integrity or that of their organization in order to win. We've all seen countless examples of this. From fudging success rates in clinical trials to the Boeing Max 737 debacle, they are all fueled by the internal pressure to win at all costs. Their impatience and drive for outcomes leads them to accelerate too quickly, to try to do too much, without proper checks and balances. Knowing that failure is not an option, team members may hide mistakes from this leader, and they are more likely to cover up problems so as to not disappoint.

Feelings get in the way of being efficient, so this leader has little time to build the caring connection necessary to build a strong cultural foundation. The result is that if the organization is "winning," people will stay for the financial rewards, but if the organization is hit by something that causes it to struggle, people will jump ship just as easily. They will have no loyalty or deep relationships that encourage them to stay and see the challenge through.

When Michael engaged in self-development work to uncover his internal playlist, he discovered that his workaholic tendencies gave him a false sense of being in control. His underlying driver is that, if he can just outrun the competition by being more efficient, getting more done—he'll win.

I get it. Working hard and persevering may contribute to winning—whatever that means to you. But it's not the only thing. Tim Ferriss expertly turned that mindset on its head with *The 4-Hour Workweek*.[1] I'd call success in four hours a week working smarter, not working harder.

What helped Michael shift his thinking was his willingness to get curious about his pattern and obsession. To do that, he had to catch himself before he dove right into the next item on the to-do list. He needed to take a beat and ask himself: *Now why do I feel I must finish this task rather than taking care of myself or my family? What am I hoping I will feel when this next project is done? Will I really let myself feel that when I do actually accomplish this?*

He kept a journal on his desk and would take two to three minutes after finishing a task to jot down how he was feeling. He noticed that he felt a momentary exhilaration upon completion, but it wouldn't last more than three seconds before his mind went on to the next task. "I'm in a virtual hamster wheel!" he exclaimed. "And I realize my work is like a drug. But the high isn't lasting as long as it used to and I just keep going and going hoping it will. I need to get off the hamster wheel."

Through applying the playlist process, he saw that he seeks out the short-term dopamine hit of crossing something off his list, but he's missing a whole swath of things that are also important to him, that don't get put on that list. These include being there for his son's baseball game and taking his wife out for a date night. This same narrowing drive to achieve can be a blind spot for him at work, because he doesn't slow down to allow for creativity, innovation, and brainstorming that would allow the company to evolve.

Michael's new playlist is called "I Am Loved No Matter What," and the central song is "Give Love" by Andy Grammer. It's a bubbly, happy song about spreading joy and love to all those you deeply care about. This song was meaningful to Michael because when we talked about when he felt the most love in his life, it was when he was giving love to his wife and children, spending time with them, and encouraging and supporting them. In the process of giving love, he received love. Michael was clear that this was what really mattered to him. And the high from being in this state lingered for days—much longer than the three second satisfaction he got from "winning" again.

When I've worked with executives like Michael, I know they've shifted their playlist when I hear things like "What was all this running around for?" They realize they've been on autopilot. They narrowly defined success as being able to cross things off the list. Now, their list is broader, so to speak. It includes spending more time with their family and more time roaming the halls to connect with their team, to hear their ideas and concerns. Through that low-key interaction with staff, leaders like Michael are able to make important shifts in strategy and to create additional product innovations that would not have been possible before the playlist shift.

 COMPARING PLAYLISTS

MICHAEL'S OLD PLAYLIST: "I AM LOVED ONLY IF I SUCCEED"

Anchor Song: "Winning" by Santana

SUPERPOWERS

- Dedication
- Goal orientation
- Reliability

LIABILITIES

- Workaholism
- A lack of patience
- A lack of caring connection

MICHAEL'S NEW PLAYLIST: "I AM LOVED NO MATTER WHAT"

Anchor Song: "Give Love" by Andy Grammer

For the full list of songs in Michael's playlist, both old and new, and for a document that can provide inspiration to create your own, visit www.theleadersplaylistbook.com or scan the QR code below.

7

Lonely Boy

Charlie is a CFO whose brilliant intellect helped him rise to the C-suite of a Fortune 500 technology company. Charlie initially scoffed at the leadership development program we created for the senior team, calling it "therapy" and dismissing the investment that the company was making in growing its leaders. He was, after all, the CFO, and this kind of investment felt like a waste of precious, hard-earned revenue. To the CEO, Charlie pretended that he was going along, but in our one-on-one meetings, his direct quote was "I don't see how this program is going to add one cent to our bottom line." In his mind, if you weren't spending money with a direct correlation to sales, what was the point?

Charlie loved to debate me on the relevance of the research when he got his 360 feedback. Sometimes, when leaders have a high IQ, they use their intellect as a weapon. They feel entitled to their status and position, because they think they are—and may actually be—smarter than everyone else. These leaders don't suffer fools, and their jadedness shuts down any possibility for growth. These are often the toughest cases. In their arrogance, they don't see the need to develop their EQ, because they rely so heavily on their IQ.

This type of leader can make a powerful shift if they can acknowledge the fact that the overreliance on their high IQ is a form of overprotectiveness. For Charlie, deep down, he was afraid of being taken advantage of, as his father was by his mother. Charlie's mother was, as he described it, a narcissist who refused to take responsibility for anything. She basically perfected the art of complaining, while his father desperately tried to win her affection by giving in to her demands. Charlie couldn't stand the weakness he saw in his father, although at the same time, he was very protective of him and spoke highly of him in our coaching work. But no way, no how was he going to end up like him!

Charlie embraced the drive to outsmart everyone around him. Eventually, this drive fueled his rise up the company ranks. Everyone in the workplace acknowledged his finance brilliance and agreed that he was an extraordinary contributor. But was he a good leader? That was a completely different story. No one wanted to work for him, and he had a terrible time retaining staff members. To Charlie, it was always their fault, due to their incompetence, and it was a blessing that they left. But after the third or fourth time his company lost a talented employee because of Charlie's behavior, the CEO got wise to it and delivered some harsh feedback. "I don't care how good you are," he said. "If you can't lead others, you can't stay here."

For some leaders, that's the bellyful that drives them to look under the hood and do some deeper work. For others, it's a battle cry, as it was for Charlie. "Well, I'll show you!" was essentially his strategy, because it wasn't him that was the problem; it was always everyone else. He ended up taking another position at a different tech company, where he was eventually let go when they, too, discovered his pattern of behavior.

Had Charlie not run away, but instead had the real courage to look within, he could have made significant discoveries that would have shifted his leadership and his personal relationships for the better. He could have relaxed the need to protect himself and be in fight mode, and his perception of what was occurring during interpersonal exchanges would have shifted away from the lens of being attacked.

Charlie perceived these exchanges as attacks because his underlying playlist, believe it or not, was "I Will Be Rejected." Charlie's fear of rejection led him to try to prove to everyone around him why they needed him—because he's so smart. As Charlie showed, if you give this type of person any hint that you are displeased, they are likely to leave before they are fired (whether or not they were considering that option), because they cannot face rejection. It would mean their deepest fear had become a reality. They reject you first. "I quit my job," this wounded leader says, "and will go somewhere else, where they want me. I will preemptively soothe the wound of potentially being rejected." But meanwhile, they skip out on doing the deeper work to stop this playlist from running them.

If I had been coaching Charlie (and he was willing to be coached) I would have asked him to connect to the emotions he was feeling when he got that 360 feedback. Most likely it would have been something in the realm of irritation, anger, and feeling misunderstood. Then we would have looked at what songs best represented those emotions for him—what would he connect to that had the same emotional frequency?

The song "Lonely Boy" by the Black Keys could have been a good one to capture this sentiment. Despite feeling "better than" his love interest, the song expresses the rejection of being kept waiting and taken for granted, leaving the singer lonely and rejected. We can feel the narrator's hurt and the pain of having his heart ripped out by someone's careless discarding of his affection. Being taken for granted and ignored is central to this song, and it captures the anger and feelings of rejection perfectly.

But this type of wounded leader has the superpower of insight and critical thinking. Their analytical skills and ability to discern what is needed to achieve organizational goals help others prioritize their workloads. People value their opinions, and they may use this person as a sanity check before taking action toward a particular strategy.

However, a playlist like Charlie's leads to a disconnect strategy: When things get tough or if this wounded leader senses that they are going to get a bad review, they may leave the relationship or organization before they have a chance to be rejected (either physically or emotionally). Their growth could come from using that insightful mind and high IQ to ask more questions, in an open and curious way. They might then see conflict as an opportunity for growth rather than rejection.

An intelligent leader suffering from a crippling fear of rejection feels excluded from teams and companies, and they take a lack of constant accolades as evidence of failure and eventual rejection. Given that rejection is this type of leader's worst nightmare, they will subconsciously take steps to avoid it. When things get tough, the wounded leader thinks, *If I sense you are going to give me a bad review, I'll leave before you have the chance.*

This type of leader will disengage, although you may not always see it since they know they can't hop from one company to the next without looking bad. So they stay in their role and seem like they are on board, but quietly harbor resentment and "phone it in" in terms of their engagement. It can take several years for the bosses of these leaders to recognize the loss in productivity and the lack of drive, and to connect the dots of the weak excuses for poor performance. By then, deadlines may be missed, and the team under them lacks engagement as well.

On the other end of the spectrum, a leader with this playlist may forcefully attack others, another manifestation of preemptive rejection. The fear of being rejected leads them to pump up their superiority to prove how much better they are than their peers. This manifests in arrogant, aggressive behavior. I've seen many CEOs spend endless energy dealing with the fallout of internal C-suite conflict with this type of wounded leader on the executive team. And when the CEO has to invest their energy in being the peacemaker, they can't focus on more important issues, such as meeting with new investors and key stakeholders, or strategic planning for the future.

Charlie's new playlist could have been "I Am Welcomed." This playlist is reaffirming and inclusive, represented by the song "Glad You Came" by the Wanted. It's a song of gratitude for the difference that another person is making in the narrator's life, of wanting to spend time together and hoping they stay. At its core, it's representing the primal feeling of belonging—to someone, someplace, or somewhere, which is what Charlie most wants to experience in his life.

Had Charlie understood how his playlist was running him, he could have used that powerful intellect to ask more questions, in an open, curious way, and learn more about what people were trying to accomplish rather than shutting them down. Once people felt heard, he could have then used that brilliance to suggest additional ideas to accomplish goals that perhaps didn't involve the dangers he foresaw. He could start trusting others because he could truly start trusting himself. The business would have benefitted, because it would have had a brilliant CFO who could also be highly effective with his peers and direct reports. He would have benefitted because by letting go of energetically protecting himself, he would have allowed more energy to be freed up to accept himself, bringing a type of relaxation that would have allowed him to enjoy life in a way he never had before.

As an enlightened leader (after doing the work to shift your playlist), a fear of rejection can be turned into inquisitiveness and wisdom. This leader can guide others to find their own answers, while offering them the insight of their observations and powerful questions.

COMPARING PLAYLISTS

CHARLIE'S OLD PLAYLIST: "I WILL BE REJECTED"

Anchor Song: "Lonely Boy" by the Black Keys

SUPERPOWERS

- Insight
- Analytical thinking
- Continuous improvement
- A drive toward quality

LIABILITIES

- Attacking
- Disconnection
- Being the first to pull the plug to avoid rejection
- Superiority
- Showing off to prove one's own superiority

CHARLIE'S NEW PLAYLIST: "I AM WELCOMED"

Anchor Song: "Glad You Came" by the Wanted

For the full list of songs in Charlie's playlist, both old and new, and for a document that can provide inspiration to create your own, visit www.theleadersplaylistbook.com or scan the QR code below.

8

You Say

Brandon is a newly minted manager in his late twenties at a Big Four accounting firm. He has vowed to treat his new junior staff much differently than he was treated by his manager; that is, he is running from being like his previous manager. When I work with mid-level managers, I'm always disheartened to hear about the lack of role models they have. Few of them have seen what great leadership looks like. When I ask them, "Who's the best leader you've ever worked with?," many can't say they feel like any of their previous leaders were that great. Despite the plethora of leadership books and educational leadership programs, most leaders are falling short. Instead of just running from oppressive leadership, the enlightened leader runs toward something. That something is a meaningful mission: generally to improve the lives of people or the planet. Ultimately, this higher purpose creates the space for the leader to be fully engaged in a meaningful mission that inspires you and all those around you.

Brandon wants to make sure his team has lots of feedback (which he didn't get). More specifically, he wants to give them lots of positive feedback. He wants to build deeper trust and be more communicative about specific goals and about how his team is working toward achieving those goals. These lofty and inspiring goals *feel* like they are mission-driven. However, the reality is: he is having trouble getting what he needs from his team to be successful. For instance, all that positive feedback during the year has generated an expectation in his team that they are all ready for a promotion. When Brandon isn't able to promote everyone, resentment starts building in his team, leading to disengagement. And while he wants to be more communicative about how their work fits into the company goals, he's not quite sure himself, since his manager doesn't help him connect the dots either.

Stuck between a rock and a hard place, Brandon feels the tension between wanting to be successful and wanting to be a good leader, as if he can't have both. But what's really driving Brandon is a deep-seated need to be liked. He wants to be liked by his boss and by his team. This underlying need or wound means that Brandon is not as direct as he could be with his team about where they disappoint or with his boss about what he needs from him to be successful.

The old playlist driving Brandon's need to be liked is a fundamental belief that he is inadequate. We called this playlist "I Am Not Enough." When you have this playlist stuck on repeat, you desperately need to get the people around you to like you, to prove to yourself that you are enough. But no amount of proof or approval will heal this wound; you must heal it for yourself.

If you are this type of wounded leader, you have the gift of creating connection. People are drawn to your leadership because they feel you have their back. You lead with your heart and create a sense of ease and peace because of your unique ability to enable others to see their own brilliance.

But if the old playlist is playing in the background, the need to be liked may drive you in ways you may not be conscious of. Be on the lookout for having your self-worth tied up in whether other people like and accept you. You are ultimately tying your worth to something you can't actually control. Instead, what needs to happen is for you to love and accept yourself. Give yourself the acknowledgment and acceptance you may be looking to get from others.

If this is your background playlist, then your insecurities cause you to play nice to feel better about yourself. The result of that is people don't get authentic feedback or build a sense of trust with the leader that they will tell it like it is. This causes team performance to be limited, because how can you continually improve if you don't have the accurate data to make adjustments? These leaders hang onto mediocre or poor performers for too long, not wanting to do the dirty work of firing those who are not a fit.

Interestingly, many of the bosses of these types of leaders report that they have a hard time giving this leader feedback as well because they know how sensitive they are. When they hear constructive criticism, they are hearing it through the filter of perceived inadequacy. It is as if it's confirming their worst nightmare. So just as their team members aren't getting direct feedback, often these leaders aren't getting it either because others treat them with kid gloves. Overall this leads to mediocre performance for the individual, the organization, and the team.

Because data about performance is being neutered, it's very difficult for these organizations to adapt and innovate. These leaders don't want to hear the bad data or communicate it to others, and therefore they can't make the necessary adjustments that the external environment (competitors, vendors, government) is pressuring them to make.

When Brandon took the ride to do the work on himself, he started to see that his need to be liked was driving him in ways he was not conscious of. He started to see that if his self-worth is tied up in whether other people like and accept him, he is ultimately tying his worth to something he can't control. He was giving his power away to anyone that he deemed important, because it was now in their hands how Brandon feels about himself.

The anchor song we chose for Brandon's playlist was "You Say" by Lauren Daigle. For Brandon, it represented a gut-wrenching story of how a woman has tied up her entire self-worth in the opinion of another. Even though, in this song, this other person is sending her encouraging thoughts, the fact that the singer is wholly dependent on the judgment of her worth to come from her lover, friend, parent, or whoever they are shows how deeply she has given her power away. If you are dependent on someone else to build you up, they also have the devastating power to tear you down.

Interestingly, Brandon didn't know that the song is a Christian song and that the singer is referring to God. But what the singer intends for the song and what you make the song to represent for you are two entirely different things. Music is highly personal and affects each of us differently; a song on someone's old playlist might represent the pattern they want to shift, while the very same song may be on someone else's new playlist and represent something that they want to emotionally move toward. It's about the meaning that the individual gives the song—and the corresponding emotions it creates in them.

One tool that was particularly powerful for Brandon was the "truth serum" exercise. When Brandon lamented how his team was struggling, I asked him to imagine he had taken a truth serum that removed any sugarcoating or niceties. It required him to speak the cold, honest truth. Imagining that I was one of his direct reports that he was struggling the most with, I asked him to speak to me as if he had taken that truth serum. I asked him to tell me exactly what he felt and perceived about my performance.

With this permission, Brandon unleashed exceptionally astute comments about where I (as the direct report) was strong and where I was failing. It was the most direct communication I had ever heard from him. When he was done, his whole face seemed lighter, as if the conversation had enabled him to take off a heavy load he was carrying. He said he felt freer and more powerful after having done that. I asked, "What keeps you from sharing your truth?," and it was then that he realized how much fear he had around rejection.

In the end, Brandon discovered that what *really* needed to happen was for Brandon to love and accept Brandon. All the external validation he was seeking needed to turn inward. How did Brandon start to love and accept himself? By giving himself the acknowledgment and acceptance he was looking to get from others.

He put this into practice by taking five minutes each morning and evening to reflect in a journal. The morning session focused on the question "Where can I practice my authentic self today?," and in the afternoon session he acknowledged one or two things he did really well that day (the kind of appreciation he would have liked to have had from others in the past).

Brandon's new playlist was called "I Am Amazing." All the songs are about exactly that, reminding him of all the ways he kicks ass! He chose exciting songs like "Me Too" by Meghan Trainor. This unabashedly confident song celebrates someone loving themselves for exactly who they are. Its irreverence celebrates not needing anyone else for affirmation and gratitude that this person is exactly who they are. The best part of their day is knowing that there is no one else in the world like them.

With this shift, Brandon is no longer concerned about sharing both positive and critical feedback—either to his team or his boss. He's more secure in himself, and he knows his value. And with that, he can see that the external world values him as well. His boss knows now that Brandon will be authentic in his feedback, so he seeks him out for more of his insights. His team works harder for him, because they have a much clearer understanding of the performance gap they need to close. When Brandon starts to truly give the praise to himself that he is seeking from others, his performance rises. As it turns out, he also starts getting that external praise as a result.

When Brandon was run by the fear that he was not enough or didn't belong, he did everything in his power to ensure that he was liked. This led to him not being direct both with those he reported to and with those who reported to him. He felt that he needed to do or say whatever the others wanted to hear or else they'd turn their backs on him. And still the monster chased him. The reality is that no amount of liking would heal his wound. Others could not do the work for him. These were wounds created long ago, when he felt he was "nobody's favorite" in his family. In Brandon's mind, his father clearly played favorites with his younger sister, and his mother was closer to Brandon's older brother—the firstborn son. Being stuck in the middle, he desperately wanted to be liked for his own unique qualities. Once Brandon really saw how he was continuing to stoke the wounds of his childhood in his corporate job, he created a new playlist. He learned how to show up as an enlightened and effective leader, and he was able to achieve the holy grail of getting stuff done while being an inspired leader.

As an enlightened leader, you can show others what it means to be a servant leader, to be of service to others, as the highest calling of humanity.

COMPARING PLAYLISTS

BRANDON'S OLD PLAYLIST: "I AM NOT ENOUGH"

Anchor Song: "You Say" by Lauren Daigle

SUPERPOWERS

- Connection
- Championing others
- Giving
- Empathy

LIABILITIES

- Lack of directness
- Trying to look good, saving face
- Poor communication
- Manipulation

BRANDON'S NEW PLAYLIST: "I AM AMAZING"

Anchor Song: "Me Too" by Meghan Trainor

For the full list of songs in Brandon's playlist, both old and new, and for a document that can provide inspiration to create your own, visit www.theleadersplaylistbook.com or scan the QR code below.

9

Alone

Olivia, an entrepreneur in her early thirties, felt the thrill of going out on her own and building a software company. Like many entrepreneurs, that thrill initially came from feeling driven by a purpose. She embraced her *why*, as all the books at the time were telling her to do, and she felt like she'd made it. Her company was up and running—even growing—and starting to provide a service Olivia truly believed in. However, like so many entrepreneurs who are really great at taking risks and coming up with a new service or product, Olivia had trouble scaling the organization. Even with her purpose crystal clear, it was difficult for her to turn vision into reality; leading a team just felt like a burden.

"As a child," Olivia recalled, "I was rewarded in school for being the innovator, and that required me to go off on my own and create something independently. I learned that I got more done if I did it myself. It felt faster and easier. I also knew that I couldn't really count on others to be as motivated—or, frankly, as competent as I was."

That kind of drive and willingness to take risks works effectively in an early-stage start-up, but as her company grew, Olivia found it difficult to delegate. She became overwhelmed to the point of collapse. Eventually, the private equity firm that backed her company had to replace her with a more seasoned CEO who knew how to scale and lead a team.

"It was incredibly humbling," she reflected. "I loved that company as my own baby. I was so committed to the mission and to seeing it succeed that I lost myself in the process. And I had to give it up for adoption, because I guess I wasn't the leader it needed to grow to adulthood."

Although it was too late for this start-up, Olivia realized that she needed help. She wanted to be ready to lead her next venture, so she connected with a coach. Her hope was that, by working on herself, she'd be able to keep up with the escalating change around her next start-up as it occurred. She realized that her independence was both a blessing and a curse, and if she kept using only one type of weapon to succeed, she ultimately wasn't going be dynamic enough to lead a growing company.

Through our work together, Olivia discovered that her drive to be independent was a reflection of a core belief that she was alone or would be abandoned. This playlist is all about independence, but it's also lonely. The song "Alone" by Halsey fit how she felt to a T. The singer knows that people want to connect with her, but her armor to protect herself from being hurt is too strong. She would rather be alone and lonely than risk exposure and get hurt in the process. This is exactly how Olivia felt about her work (and personal life). In "Alone," the singer makes the choice to run away and feels some semblance of protection, but in the melody, we hear how she ultimately feels isolated and sad. For Olivia, taking a risk to depend on others feels much scarier than being overwhelmed and doing it all herself.

Olivia recalled, "Both my parents had hard jobs and seemed to barely make time for me. They felt guilty about it, but that didn't change their behavior. I learned at a young age that if I wanted something, I was going to have to get it for myself. From learning how to make myself dinner at age six to soothing myself that it was okay that my parents didn't show up for the chorale concerts I was in."

Olivia's self-reliance became a source of pride, and it fueled and motivated her to excel. It provided a benefit that she clung to tightly as she moved through her career. Her internal drive and motivation allowed her to excel. As an independent thinker, she was able to see opportunity where others may not have, which made her particularly well suited for entrepreneurial activities. Others might describe a leader listening to this playlist as a self-starter. Some of Olivia's peers marveled at her self-determination and grit.

If you suffer from a wound like Olivia's, you may have trouble scaling an organization, because leading a team can feel oppressive. Relying on others can feel risky or frustrating. You may have learned you get more done if you do it yourself; it feels faster and easier to just get it done. You may also believe that others are not as motivated or competent, which can reinforce your drive to be independent. Opening yourself up to depending on others will be central to your growth.

Leaders repeating this playlist in the background believe that they must go it alone, because in their mind, they *are* alone. A typical consequence is poor delegation, which has a number of implications. First, this leader becomes overwhelmed and suffers from work–life balance issues. They feel they must do it all themselves, that no one else has the skill or drive to do it the way they can. Second, they become a bottleneck in the organization, slowing down throughput because they can't seem to leverage their team. This limits the ability to scale quickly, especially for early-stage companies. Third, others don't develop and grow the way they should because this leader hoards the development opportunities for themselves. In addition, they don't grow because they don't have the time to take on new opportunities or explore bigger opportunities because they keep doing the same work in front of them.

Another impact of hyperindependence is poor communication. If you believe that you are all alone, you don't make the effort to communicate the status of your work to others. You may not realize how others are affected by your behavior. This is, of course, frustrating to your coworkers. I have seen some companies hemorrhage employees who find the lack of trust in their work frustrating, and this ultimately creates a talent drain.

To Olivia, letting go of her independence would mean that all her efforts would be focused outward, supporting others and helping her team members grow. That might seem all positive, but to someone healing from this wound, it can be terrifying. Because she can't rely on anyone but herself, it means that there would be no one to take care of her. Even when it's clear that she needs to let go of the independence, to start to delegate and rely on her team, her fears rear up so strongly that she simply cannot do it.

Olivia and I did some work around her "lost childhood message." I had her recall a specific time in her life where she felt all alone and couldn't count on anyone. She told me a story about being a teen at after-school chorale practice. She sang exceptionally well that day and felt excited about performing in an upcoming concert that weekend. But her enthusiasm waned as she witnessed her classmates get picked up by their parents one by one, leaving her alone and waiting, feeling frustrated that she wasn't being cared for like her friends were. And while other parents offered her a ride, she stubbornly sat down to wait for her mom.

"I didn't want to give them an 'out,'" she said of her parents. "I wanted them to feel bad because I felt so bad." And, she continued, "I vowed to myself, as soon as I can drive, I'm never depending on them again."

I asked her to describe the belief that laid beneath her feelings about the neglect she felt from her parents and it was "I can only count on me."

"And now, seeing how that belief has been a gift and a curse in your life, if you could go back and tell little Olivia one thing that you know now, that you wished you had known then, what would it be?" I asked.

"Well, in that example, I wasn't entirely alone. Our music director stayed and waited with me, and we actually had a great conversation that night. He was really inspiring and gave me some advice that helped me with my performance that weekend."

"So it wasn't all that bad?"

"No. I guess it wasn't."

"And what do you see now that you didn't then?"

"It takes a village."

"What do you mean by that?"

"I've been so focused on not getting that support from that one person, but other people stepped in to fill the gap. I've actually not really been alone."

As Olivia began to see how her old playlist was running her life, she became aware of the wide range of choices she had. Instead of automatic self-protection, she could choose from a variety of reactions to the company's growth. Her new playlist would be filled with songs like "It Takes Two" by Rob Base and DJ E-Z Rock or "Together" by Sia. These songs celebrate the power of connection and collaboration and show how much more a team or a couple can create than any one person can independently. Her playlist title became "It Takes a Village," and she included songs about teamwork and people showing up for one another when they needed it most. Indeed, Olivia started to pay attention to all the ways people had shown up and supported her, instead of focusing on the times she felt alone or had to go it alone. The more she practiced the vibration of connection by listening to her playlist that evoked that emotional state, the more she saw helping hands outreached wherever she looked.

Olivia found that she started asking for help and didn't feel ashamed about it. Relying on her team didn't mean she wasn't competent to do the work; it meant she was a competent leader. Allowing others to contribute could be something she felt proud of rather than fearful of. She developed skills to be a better delegator, but having the right mindset about it was the crucial first step. She took those new skills and integrated them into her role as a leader. She hired people that were actually better than her at their jobs. She realized that they were the experts at their work, and she trusted them to do it. This meant that she did not feel threatened by their suggestions for changes and improvements. And because she was genuinely interested in their perspectives, her staff felt more engaged in working at the company. With their ideas getting implemented, they felt valued and engaged, and the company soared in its market. When the board gathers feedback from her team about Olivia's performance, they see the insightful collaborator she has become, and they trust that, if she continues to listen to her team and hire well, she'll be able to scale with the company.

As an enlightened leader, you will model a responsible—as opposed to a victim—mindset. You'll inspire others to hold themselves accountable for generating their own success and happiness.

COMPARING PLAYLISTS

OLIVIA'S OLD PLAYLIST: "I AM ALONE"

Anchor Song: "Alone" by Halsey

SUPERPOWERS

- Self-starting
- Independence
- Grit
- Dedication

LIABILITIES

- Poor delegation
- A lack of collaboration
- A lack of communication
- Keeping secrets

OLIVIA'S NEW PLAYLIST: "IT TAKES A VILLAGE"

Anchor Songs: "It Takes Two" by Rob Base and DJ E-Z Rock and "Together" by Sia

For the full list of songs in Olivia's playlist, both old and new, and for a document that can provide inspiration to create your own, visit www.theleadersplaylistbook.com or scan the QR code below.

10

Don't Let Me Get Me

S arah is a chief marketing officer in her late forties at a growing national retail clothing business. Well, the company *was*
growing, until COVID-19 hit. She once felt excited about her
future, but now she can't sleep with the fear that is consuming her. She
hides this fear under a veneer of cheerleading with her team, but she
doesn't realize that her constant "rah rah" attitude comes across as inau-
thentic. Her team is losing trust just when they need to pull together
to deal during a crisis.

This isn't the first time Sarah has approached conflict and challenge
in her life by masking her emotions. When she dove into coaching, her
deeper exploration showed that she had learned at an early age to hide
her vulnerability. Instead, she would show a tough side and confidence
that says, "I've got this!" even if she didn't actually feel that way.

Sarah's mother was a cold woman who was repulsed by displays
of weakness. "Toughen up," she would retort when Sarah started to

cry. "The world doesn't care!" Sarah learned that she must suppress her own vulnerability if she wanted to be successful. She despised her own perceived weakness and reacted even more strongly when she saw it in others. Secretly, she shared her frustration with the younger workers on her team. She believed that "millennials are so lazy!" and that they need to "be just like I am. Nobody gave me a trophy for participation!" But her anxiety kept following her, even though she had risen through the ranks to the dream job she'd always wanted.

She believed that, if she faked it until she made it, the anxiety and fear would go away with that eventual success. Like many leaders, she thought that reaching a pinnacle of her career would provide happiness. But when she got there, she only found more stress and unhappiness than she had ever experienced before. In her more lucid moments, she connected to an incredible sense of loneliness that came from being at the top, from not knowing who she could trust and who was using her. Until she could look deeper at the playlist running her life and consciously choose a new, more empowering one, she wouldn't be able to build the kind of leadership skills that were required to lead her team.

Deep down, she was repeating a playlist we called "I Am an Imposter." The anchor song we used for her playlist was Pink's "Don't Let Me Get Me." For Sarah, it was a song that represented someone not really liking who they were and who felt the need and desire to be someone else. Annoyed by herself, like the narrator in the song, Sarah would perceive that as annoyance by others. For example, she would criticize millennials, when it was actually Sarah who didn't like Sarah. Pink's song is about being your own worst enemy to the point of being an actual hazard to yourself. With Sarah's imposter syndrome running wild, she was not only a hazard to herself but to others, too.

If you are this kind of leader, who fears they are an imposter, you have the gift of versatility and the ability to rally the troops to do what is needed to be successful. Others gravitate to your energy, enthusiasm, and perseverance. A natural cheerleader, you inspire others to believe in themselves and in the success of your team.

But there are all sorts of overprotective behaviors that can show up when we feel differently inside than what we think the outside world expects of us, including defensiveness, arrogance, and extreme optimism. Consequently, if this playlist is repeating in your background, you may approach conflict and challenge in your life by masking your emotions. That inauthenticity will limit your leadership effectiveness by creating disillusionment in your team over time. When you have done the inner work to believe in yourself, you will inspire confidence in others through being comfortable in your own skin.

This type of leader ultimately doesn't feel like they can be themselves in the workplace. They must morph to be what others want them to be, and in the process they create an energy of inauthenticity. The fear of being found out, that they "aren't that good" or "don't deserve to have this position," can create coping behaviors that drive the leader to show off to convince those around them that they are the real deal. And if they can convince others, perhaps they can convince themselves. The result is an inability to admit mistakes. They actively cover their mistakes because if someone sees their vulnerability, it will confirm their worst fears of being inadequate. The cover-up is often worse than the crime. If a leader can't admit their mistakes, they certainly can't fix them.

In Sarah's case, she knows she has to be the leader, she has to be strong, but deep down she feels anxious and scared. Not liking those feelings, she pushes these thoughts way down and covers them up with cheerleading. She is trying to convince herself as much as anyone else.

When she accepted the challenge to change her playlist, she used her grit to do the real courageous work she needed to do on the inside. Eventually, she found the inner peace she was longing for.

She discovered that her bravado was a form of self-soothing. She was attempting to prove to herself that she was tough as nails, as if that would somehow keep adversity at bay. By understanding the inner playlist running her, she understood that the tough exterior was just a mask, and she was expending a lot of energy to wear it day in and day out. It was this exhaustion that gave her the motivation to find a different way.

"What do you want to be feeling instead of exhausted and 'performing' all the time?" I asked her.

"I want to feel confident, secure, and in love with myself."

"Then let's build the playlist that gets you into that emotional state. Your homework is to find songs that, as you listen to them, allow you to access feelings of confidence and loving yourself." And off she went in search of her new state of being.

Sarah's new playlist title is "I Am Free to Be Me." The more she practices this emotional state, the less she feels the need to hide behind bubbly optimism. Instead, she embraces her real talents and admits her shortcomings. Then she learns and grows to address those shortcomings to turn them into strengths. The song "Good as Hell" by Lizzo was her anchor song in her new playlist. It's a powerful tune about saying "fuck you" to anyone who doesn't like you and celebrating your own amazing soul. It's about feeling good no matter what people think, no matter if your lover doesn't love you anymore. This song made Sarah want to get up and dance, and the boldness of the lyrics and melody kept her feeling the confidence and love for herself that she wanted to continue to emanate. As she went into a meeting where she would normally put her imposter face on, she remembered Lizzo singing and shifted her state immediately. Sarah is good enough. She is free to be exactly who she is in the moment.

Once she stopped running from or covering up her "monster"

emotions, Sarah instead turned to look them in the eye. She discovered that true strength means showing your vulnerabilities to others. That required the real courage that she had been afraid to access. Through showing vulnerability, as well as strength, she became more approachable, more human, and more likely to connect and inspire her team to work harder. And as she showed her vulnerability, others felt safe to share theirs, and that's where she could truly lead.

She now supports her younger team members where they feel weak instead of judging them as lazy. They know she has their back, so they have hers. Just like that, the loneliness from being at the top dissipated. Sarah's personal evolution is her leadership evolution, and the results are: the team is on fire and it harnesses all its resources on the mission of the company.

COMPARING PLAYLISTS

SARAH'S OLD PLAYLIST: "I AM AN IMPOSTER"

Anchor Song: "Don't Let Me Get Me" by Pink

SUPERPOWERS

- Versatility
- Enthusiasm
- Perseverance
- Strength

LIABILITIES

- Being a slick salesman

- Behaving like a chameleon, constantly changing with the situation
- Having trouble building trust
- Overconfidence masking a lack of confidence
- Avoidance of vulnerability
- Inauthenticity

SARAH'S NEW PLAYLIST: "I AM FREE TO BE ME"

Anchor Song: "Good as Hell" by Lizzo

For the full list of songs in Sarah's playlist, both old and new, and for a resource that can provide inspiration to create your own, visit www.theleadersplaylistbook.com or scan the QR code below.

11

Flaws

G reg was the COO of a private equity firm, and he ran a tight
ship. He felt an enormous sense of responsibility to ensure
that everything ran smoothly and that everyone had what
they needed to be successful. These are wonderful leadership qualities,
but when they are grounded in the leader's ego, it's not so much about
the firm winning as it is about *the leader* winning.

"Prickly" is how Greg's colleagues described him. He was incredibly
detail-oriented, a perfectionist, and committed to creating structured
processes and protocols within the firm. His colleagues trusted that he
could get the job done and do it right. But they would avoid interacting
with him as much as possible. "I get this pit in my stomach every time
I have to engage him," said one of his team members. "He's just not a
fun guy to talk to."

Greg was ruthlessly efficient with his time. If he decided that one of his employees came to a meeting unprepared, he'd rip into them for their lack of consideration for his busy schedule. He attempted to hide it under a veneer of politeness, which just came across as passive-aggressive. In management committee meetings, he would also throw darts of judgment at colleagues he deemed "idiots" or "slackers." The head of the firm said, "I love what he produces, but his bedside manner could use some improvement so we don't have all this shrapnel."

So why was Greg so angry? Why couldn't he believe that anyone else was as responsible as he was? Was it really about them being poor performers? Or was there something else driving Greg to get so triggered by perceived incompetence? Exploring his childhood wounds, where it all began, was illuminating. We started by focusing on how he was feeling in the present. I asked him about the last time he was triggered by something at work. He was able to share an event that happened just the day before, when he heard secondhand about a colleague's plans that seemed to conflict with his own agenda. I asked him to tune in to the emotions he felt as this incident unfolded.

"I'm annoyed and frustrated! These people don't know what they are doing!" he shared. After empathizing with his situation, I asked how often he feels this same pattern of emotions—annoyed and frustrated.

"Around here? Almost daily! Well maybe it's not that bad but probably a couple of times a week."

"That seems like a lot of energy spent in frustration. How is that for you?"

"It sucks! I don't want to be annoyed all the time."

"Sounds like you have a pattern, or playlist, going there. Would you be open to exploring where that began?"

Greg agreed, and I asked him to connect to the earliest memory he had of feeling annoyed and frustrated. "Oh!" he exclaimed, "that happened a lot!"

It turns out that his mother was an alcoholic, his dad was a philanderer, and, eventually, his younger brother became an alcoholic as well. "My childhood was a shit show," he shared. "I felt like I had to be the parent in our family and felt like I never really had the chance to be a kid. Sometimes my mother would leave me at basketball practice and forget to pick me up. As I was the last team member there, I would try to hide my shame to the coach, who was also waiting for me to go home. Eventually, he had to take me back."

Believe it or not, this is a more common storyline than you might think. How you react to the perceived abandonment can influence the playlist. Greg explained, "I'd come home to find my mother passed out on the couch and my brother eating M&Ms for dinner. At ten years old, I would be the one to make him dinner—mac and cheese, of course—and to put a blanket around my mother to sleep it off. And my dad? He was out fucking some floozy somewhere, so he really didn't give a shit."

No wonder Greg felt so much responsibility to take care of everything at the firm. He had been groomed for that role his whole life. And while that can be a blessing, it can also foster deep resentment. His colleagues were now the surrogate targets for his underlying resentment of his parents. Every time the head of human resources or the director of accounting made a misstep, it was as if Greg's mother was leaving him at basketball practice again. Until he heals that massive wound, everyone else is going to feel the impatience and seething irritation. And Greg's compensation will continue to suffer because he's creating so much "shrapnel" at the firm.

You might be asking how we can heal wounds that deep. We heal them the same way I had to heal the wounds of a rage-aholic father. We follow the process to forgive (not forget) so that we can stop injecting ourselves with the poison of hatred. "You have every right to be angry at your parents," I said. "However, we need to explore what that is doing to *you*. Is it changing their behavior?"

Greg realized he had stuffed a lot of his anger down, but he couldn't keep the lid on it, and it came out by scalding others. Thankfully, he realized he needed help. He embraced journaling and wrote and wrote and wrote. He wrote about his anger, about his resentment for having to parent himself and his brother, and even about his anger that it was affecting his job now. He was surprised to experience how cathartic it was. "I thought about sending some of it to her, but then I thought, *What's the point?* I'm not doing this for her, because she isn't changing. I did this for me." Alongside journaling, he started to identify songs that best represented this pent-up frustration—his original playlist, which revealed and represented his wound.

Generally, leaders of this type are proud that they can be counted on to get it done and get it done right. They are excellent producers and usually rise through the ranks because of this gift. Greg's wounded playlist is "I Have to Be Perfect." He required that strict perfectionism of himself so that he wouldn't end up messing things up as badly as his parents did.

What these leaders don't realize is that they use their belief in their superiority to fuel their drive. Usually at a young age, they learned they could count on themselves and couldn't really count on others in the same way. Their resentment of others' perceived lack of responsibility leaks through in the wounded leader's leadership. If there is a belief that others won't show up at their best—as had been proven to Greg and me at an early age—then we're on the lookout for how others are not carrying their weight, not doing it the right way, not nearly as "good" as we are.

This wounded leader is especially good at taking a vision and turning it into reality by organizing work and people to accomplish the mission. They are admired for helping others get unstuck, because they always seem to know what the next best step should be in any process. With this playlist on in the background, you may feel an enormous sense of responsibility to ensure that everything runs smoothly and that everyone has what they need to be successful.

Inevitably, that kind of pressure cooker can take its toll on you. You may lash out with impatience or frustration, causing others to recoil from your criticism. Your perfectionism causes you to spend too much time to complete projects. In your attempts to avoid failure (which to the perfectionist includes even minor errors), you get behind schedule. Working toward unattainable perfection wastes a lot of time and it slows innovation and time to market. These leaders often have trouble prioritizing; everything is equally important, and they can burn out their team by constantly iterating to get it right.

Perfectionism also dampens the willingness of the team to take risks or find their own path to solve a problem. The direct reports of perfectionist leaders become dependent on them to tell them exactly what they want so they don't disappoint and are forced to deal with their boss's irritation and resentment. The consequence is that the team doesn't grow and learn to trust their own judgment, and the organization is faced with a key-person risk situation: if that leader is hit by a bus, there is no one in the department who has built up the skill set or confidence to take over.

But you are the DJ of your own playlist. You can replace the songs that remind you of resentment or perfection and instead play something supportive. Greg's new playlist was called "I Am Loved for My Flaws," and he embraced that sense of beauty in imperfection. We focused on the reasons for change: Greg's bellyful of annoyance and frustration.

He'd recently been diagnosed with high blood pressure and was on prescription meds, which he hated. I sent him a significant amount of research that details how your emotional state affects your health. Given that Greg, by his own admission, was getting frustrated to varying degrees several times a week, if not every day, he was sending a cascade of stress hormones into his body on a regular basis. No wonder his body was starting to send clear signals that this emotional pattern wasn't serving him. He was ready for change—and, thankfully, before a more significant health issue like a heart attack would be the wake-up call.

He wanted to catch himself and shift sooner, before he got "hypnotized" by the old emotional pattern of being frustrated and irritated. Trying to do that logically, by telling himself that what he was annoyed by wasn't important or that he should just stop getting upset didn't work. The rational mind had plenty of arguments on the other side, repeating all the reasons he should be frustrated. We needed to bypass this pattern, and music was the conduit.

We identified the anchor song for his old playlist as "Flaws" by Bastille. The artist references a deep hole in his soul that he struggles to fill and how he tries to hide his flaws by burying them deep beneath the ground. For Greg, that was the reminder of the cost of his stuffed-down anger and how that was literally making him sick.

"Everyone has flaws, and so do I," he would exclaim to me. "It's time I start accepting those in myself and others."

Getting to know his wound by creating its playlist, Greg says, "enabled me to catch myself when I noticed the frustration welling in me. I would think of one of the songs and say, 'Oh, here I go again.' And then I would shift into the new place, which is to ask for what I need and feel grateful for receiving it—even before I would physically ask. It changed my demeanor; I found people much more willing to meet me at least halfway."

At the end of the year, as I collected feedback on Greg from his colleagues, I heard things like "He definitely wins the award for most improved player. He has so much talent, but his attitude was atrocious. Now, he actually feels like a partner, and I'm not so nervous when we engage."

Would you be surprised to hear that the perfect song Greg chose for his new playlist was "All of Me" by John Legend? It's a beautiful love song about one person's love for another, with all their imperfections. And Greg chose that, not so much to remind him to love others unconditionally but to love himself that way. To love himself in his imperfections was the biggest opportunity for change. If he loved himself, then he could be more tolerant and welcoming to others. The reality is that how you treat others is how you treat yourself. If we were going to make changes in Greg's leadership, it had to start with the most important relationship he will ever have: his relationship with himself.

"Seek, and ye shall find." This is one of the most powerful phrases in the Bible (Matthew 7:7 KJV). It illuminates the fact that where our perception goes, our attention follows. The perfectionist wound ultimately becomes isolating in a team setting. Greg's colleagues hid failures to avoid having his scathing judgment rained down upon them for their sins. The perfectionist leader's team members are drained by the constant criticism, and over time they withdraw, further leaving that wounded leader to pick up the pieces—and further justifying their beliefs. The type of engagement and collaboration between departments that is necessary to run a successful organization is thwarted by the shrapnel of the superiority complex of one leader. Until we heal the wounded leader, that shrapnel causes even more wounds.

As an enlightened leader (if you do the work to shift your playlist), you can bring clarity and assurance that the vision can be accomplished by breaking things down into a road map that everyone can follow.

COMPARING PLAYLISTS

GREG'S OLD PLAYLIST: "I HAVE TO BE PERFECT"

Anchor Song: "Flaws" by Bastille

SUPERPOWERS

- Structuring and organizing a path to success
- Taking responsibility seriously
- Problem-solving skills

LIABILITIES

- Criticizing others and themselves
- Tenseness
- Irritation
- Resentment of others
- Scathing anger

GREG'S NEW PLAYLIST: "I AM LOVED FOR MY FLAWS"

Anchor Song: "All of Me" by John Legend

For the full list of songs in Greg's playlist, both old and new, and for a resource that can provide inspiration to create your own, visit www.theleadersplaylistbook.com or scan the QR code below.

12

Putting a Playlist into Practice

You now have a basic philosophical grasp of how a playlist can represent a leader's wound or their healed state. You may start to recognize your own wound and how you might change it. Here's a real-world practical guide to how to find your new playlist title and your own songs of healing. A good coach can help you crystallize it. They'll help you learn how to ask the right questions and will help you home in on what the exact title is that would best shift that old neural pathway. It's different for everyone, but I've come up with a seven-step process of statements and questions that helped me and that I have used to help many others. I walk you through the process just as if I were coaching you in person. If you would like to get a summary of this process with the key questions I suggest you use to help you change your playlist, scan the QR code below. Ready? Let's go!

Step 1: Get a Bellyful

A dear friend and former roommate introduced this phrase to me to describe when you reach your limit with the status quo: you've got a bellyful. Sometimes it takes decades to get a bellyful. For some people, it's stepping on that scale and seeing a number higher than they have ever seen before. Sometimes it's deep suffering. Whatever it is, we realize that our environment or the frequency we are broadcasting isn't working anymore. Unfortunately, we often need to reach a level of deep suffering before we realize we need to make changes in our lives. I wish that wasn't the case, but it seems that, without deep pain, our subconscious loves the status quo. If you don't have a true bellyful, you won't have the courage or inclination to do the deep work that the next steps require.

When you've finally had enough, ask yourself these questions:

- What are you no longer willing to tolerate in your life?
- Have you truly had a bellyful, such that you are willing to dive deep and uncover the playlist running your life?

DEBORAH GETS A BELLYFUL

An executive I recently coached, Deborah, got her bellyful in the form of feedback she received from her colleagues: that she was aggressively trying to involve herself in projects that others felt were in their area of responsibility. From her perspective, she felt like she was being left out of important conversations that affected her division.

Both are possibly true. However, in my experience, it's not what's going on now but what went on long ago that keeps showing up in different forms in our lives. We'll delve into that, but for this first step, all that needs to happen is that you reach your rock bottom. For Deborah, that was being passed over for a promotion that she really wanted, with her boss delivering some challenging feedback in her year-end review.

If you haven't had a bellyful, you are unlikely to take the steps to make changes. The body and the mind generally don't like change. They work hard to maintain the status quo, even if it is not in our best interest. Did Deborah want to continue to live in this pattern? As is frequently the case, she was almost ready, but she needed the second step for it to really hit home.

Step 2: Get Curious

Judgment says, "I know how it is," and the moment that happens, we shut down the ability to take in new information. Judgment is the secure safe haven, the home base. It's what the body wants to feel: security and knowing. You almost feel a sense of relief when you can say, "Ah, I know this. I understand it, and this is how the world works."

Curiosity is the opposite of judgment. Curiosity says, "There

115

is something more here for me to learn, and I am open to receive it." Curiosity is the adventurer. It means you have to leave your safe place of "I know how it is!" for the unknown of "Hey, maybe there is more to it."

Curiosity and judgment are opposite ends of the spectrum, and we all have the opportunity to toggle between them, back and forth along that spectrum. Much of the business writing out there is filled with judgment, the "I know better than you, so here it is." While I can outline a process for others to take this adventure, I can't go on the adventure for you. Your mode of transportation will be your own curiosity, if you have the courage to look.

What stops people (including me) from going on the curiosity adventure is the penchant for beating yourself up. I was certainly prone to beating myself up for the things that went wrong in my life. While that is a step above making it everyone else's fault (the victim mindset, which I also had at certain moments), it still keeps you in the place of judgment. And it means you've tuned in to the wrong song. You have to get curious and ask yourself the deeper questions. It's not "That's just who I am" but "Who am I really?"

At its core, you have to have the curiosity to really look at what you are running away from. I was running away from being my dad—angry and lashing out. I didn't need my dad to do that for me; I learned how to do it myself. In times of stress, I often turned to blaming, to being angry, and to lashing out at myself. On and on the playlist played. I didn't even realize that music was playing in the background. I was finally able to create space for curiosity. Without embracing curiosity, I wasn't ever going to be able to create a different outcome in my life.

When you're ready to get curious, ask yourself the following questions:

- Where do you need to give up what you think you know and get curious about why and how patterns are showing up in your life?

- Where is blaming yourself or others (a.k.a. your judgment) getting in the way of your curiosity?

DEBORAH GETS CURIOUS

In the beginning of our work together, Deborah held a lot of defensiveness about her version of the story. I get it; we are all attached to our stories. It is the familiar playlist, reinforcing the neural pathways that we groove into our psyche for decades. We can't hear any other songs over that core music. Like a behavioral earworm, the song is stuck in our head.

Deborah went into great detail about how "they" just didn't get it. The business would function far better if "they" were more inclusive, resulting in better collaboration. "They"—and there is always a "they" when you are stuck in a playlist—were her peers. In her view, the CFO was trying to make her look bad and to make himself look better when he tore into her financial reports during a team meeting. The chief human resource officer was handcuffing her from hiring better talent into her department when she insisted that the HR team needed to do all the initial candidate screenings. But the worst of all was Ned, another division president. He purposefully left her out of key strategic meetings that ultimately affected the work she was doing with their joint customers.

Rationally, it all sounded very convincing. But I'm not coaching "them," so I can't do anything about changing her colleagues' mindsets. Deborah came to our coaching frustrated. She wanted help being a stronger leader with more influence on her peers. Basically, she wanted help crafting the most persuasive language for how she could get her environment to change. Instead, I redirected her to explore why this type of situation showed up in her life in the first place. What if the thing she had to change was her internal environment, not the external one?

Step 3: Tune into the Melody of Emotions

By the very nature of the senior leadership work that I do, a disproportionate number of my clients are men. Many of them find tapping into and naming their emotions incredibly hard. I often provide a list of about a hundred different emotions they might be feeling and have them circle up to five that fit. This helps them find the language to name the frequency of their playlist. Usually, they are astounded by this.

"How can there be so many different emotions?" they ask. "And I have to choose only five? I didn't realize the nuance could be so important, but it feels much better to be precise with what I'm feeling. This is much better than a generalized 'angry' or 'sad.'"

The distinction here is similar to the options on your car for listening to music. You have options for FM, AM, satellite radio, or connecting your iPhone. Think of these as the seven core emotions: anger, anxiety, fear, love, joy, sadness, and shame. Once you delve into the FM stations or your iPhone, you have further choices: 99.5 FM or your favorite Yacht Rock playlist. It's important to know exactly what station you are on and in what mode of play, because if you don't like the music, you will have a better shot of changing to a different station. Knowing your emotional station helps you identify your pattern of behavior, and it can help you determine the playlist of your life, the background music you've been playing all along.

Here's a sample of what I'm talking about in terms of granularity, adapted from the coaching organization Learning in Action.[1] The words highlighted in gray represent the recurring playlist I had tuned in to, which had the core emotions of anger, fear, and shame.

ANGER	ANXIETY	FEAR	LOVE	JOY	SADNESS	SHAME
Agitated	Confused	Alarmed	Attention	Alive	Crushed	Ashamed
Anger	Distant	Defensive	Caring	Bold	Disappointed	Burdened
Annoyed	Dread	Doubtful	Comforting	Brave	Discouraged	Condemned
Appalled	Dulled	Dread	Compassion	Capable	Distraught	Despised
Disgusted	Frantic	Fearful	Encouraged	Confident	Distressed	Disgraced
Frustrated	Helpless	Frightened	Engaged	Curious	Empty	Embarrassed
Irritated	Impatient	Reluctant	Gentle	Delighted	Grief	Guilty
Outraged	Intense	Suspicious	Honored	Dynamic	Lonely	Humiliated
Spiteful	Nervous	Tense	Open	Eager	Lost	Inadequate
Upset	Numb	Worried	Respect	Elated	Miserable	Isolated
Vindictive	Overwhelmed	Victimized	Secure	Energized	Resigned	Outcast/Left out
	Paralyzed	Jealousy	Tender	Glad	Sadness	Regretful
	Perplexed		Gratitude	Hopeful		Shame
	Skeptical		Blessed	Joyful		
	Stressed		Love	Optimistic		
	Uneasy			Passionate		
				Peaceful		
				Safe		

Men aren't the only ones who, through upbringing and conditioning, may have adapted to downplay their emotions and their emotional life. I've seen plenty of women, including myself, do the same. There is a belief that it's not personal—it's just business—as though we could leave emotions out of the business world and everything would run fine. The reality is that emotions are central in business and in any other aspect of life.

To tune in to your emotions, ask yourself the following questions:

- As you connect to the part of your life where you have a bellyful, what emotions are you feeling right now?
- What frequency (low or high) are those emotions? Name them with as much specificity as possible.

DEBORAH TUNES IN TO HER MELODY OF EMOTIONS

To work through the process of tuning in to her melody of emotions, Deborah started by clarifying the emotions that came up for her during one of her work conflicts.

This is such an important exercise—to name the emotion. Emotions are not good or bad in themselves. In fact, they are extremely helpful to give us information. But we tend to gloss over them, choosing instead to point our attention to that colleague or work situation or home situation that's creating a negative experience. We need to turn that attention inward.

When she accessed her own state of emotions, she connected to anger and then jealousy. As we delved into the anger part first, I had her identify how that shows up in her interactions. More specifically, what form of anger does she feel? She said that, most often, she felt irritation and frustration as her root emotion of anger took hold. Then we looked at the jealousy and discussed how, at its root, it's a form of fear. She was afraid that she wouldn't get what others are getting, that somehow it would either be taken away or withheld from her. She hadn't quite realized how much fear was actually driving her, but connecting to the root emotion enabled her to dig deeper in the next step.

Step 4: Name the Playlist through Your Earliest Memory

Of course, we are meant to experience and express a wide range of emotions. Emotions are our guidance system. What we often don't realize, though, is that we repeat certain ones as a favorite playlist. Our work is to dig down. Try to uncover when you felt those root emotions before, and document as many experiences as you can remember.

I initially thought my own core of anger, fear, and shame had taken over two or three times. But, frankly, while I was writing this book, taking a detailed account of my work and personal life, I began to see just how far down the rabbit hole this playlist had taken me. To do this, I looked by decade: early childhood (ages one to ten), my teenage years (ten to twenty), early adulthood (twenty to thirty), my thirties, forties, and so on. I put myself back in that place and recalled the biggest traumatic events over that decade.

This is where I took a step back to see the bigger picture of my life, the patterns of my behavior. For me, I realized that the refrain of "I Am Treated Unfairly" created a lifetime of experiences where I felt I didn't deserve to be treated the way I had by romantic partners and work colleagues.

There are a gazillion songs about heartbreak, and we've all heard those songs a thousand times. But we still seem to be interested in hearing the newest one. That's what I did in my life, what we all do. It's as if I could write that same song a hundred different times, with different refrains, but all the same story. That is the frequency I held with my belief system and that was returned to me in my life experiences. And the fascinating thing was that I couldn't see that all these experiences were part of this playlist until I went through this process.

When you look back on your life's challenges, did you experience the same emotions you identified in step 3? If so, start to notice patterns. If not, what different emotions were present, and are there any other patterns there? These emotions can each be represented by a song, and they combine to form your wounded playlist. It's helpful to document as many emotions and patterns as you can remember so you can see the full breadth of the playlist and all the places in your life where it's been on a loudspeaker and you didn't even realize it.

Tracing things all the way back, if we are able to identify the earliest memory in which the same set of emotional patterns were encoded, it's easier to see and hear our playlist. This earliest memory of trauma created a playlist in you that may inadvertently be creating songs—experiences, emotions—that you don't want in your life anymore. For me, it was when my father unexpectedly turned into Mr. Hyde and came barreling down the stairs to threaten my perceived safety. This level of trauma was deeply encoded in my subconscious. To find the song that fit this trauma, I put myself back into the body of that little girl. I connected to what she made up about the world as a result of that fear. As I licked the snow cone while it dribbled down my hands, sobbing in between breaths, I tapped into that internal frustration. Now, I asked myself, what would I call this feeling? How would I give my young self a voice to explain her wound? For me, it was "I Am Treated Unfairly," just like Sahar.

To see your own life pattern, ask yourself these questions:

- Where and when have you felt those same emotions identified in step 3 before? Trace and identify.

- Document as many experiences as you can remember where those feelings occurred.

Then, to name your own playlist, ask yourself these questions:

- With your earliest memory, what did you say to yourself about life as a result of feeling those emotions?
- What did you say about others?
- Can you boil it down to a statement—a refrain? "I Am
_____."

DEBORAH NAMES HER PLAYLIST

What other situations in Deborah's life brought up that same pattern of irritation and frustration (anger) or jealousy (fear)? She realized she had the same feeling when her kids were having fun with her ex-husband. He had cheated on her, and she left the marriage. In her mind, any time her kids enjoyed being with their father, it brought up the anger and jealousy again. Most of the time, she just stuffed it down, but sometimes it came out in weird ways, such as being passive-aggressive with them about when and where she would spend time with them. This behavior was starting to create a rift between her and her kids.

An internal dialogue pervaded her thinking: *Why is he getting to take them to the lake house over Thanksgiving? What can I tempt them with so they want to be with their mom more than their dad?* She was careful never to say this kind of thing aloud. Emotions are the language of the heart, however, and you can't hide them. As careful as she was, her kids could sense it, and they started to avoid discussing their activities with their dad—they didn't want to trigger her. But when Deborah found out about their "secret" plans, it only compounded the hurt.

She also heard that same song when she was in college. During sorority rush, she had her eye on joining Delta Gamma, the most popular, most coveted sorority on campus. Not only did she not get an invitation to that sorority; she didn't get an invitation to her second choice, either. Relegated to her third choice, she joined reluctantly but then chose to pursue other campus interests away from Greek life. While she initially poo-pooed this as just a "coming of age" story, when she really connected back to the emotion of that experience, she realized how angry she was over it, how left out she felt, and how jealous she was of those pretty DG girls.

I asked Deborah what the earliest experience she could remember was when she felt that anger and jealousy. Well, it turns out that she often felt that way with her older sister. Clara got all the attention from others when they were children, she said. Clara had beautiful blond hair, where Deborah's was "mousy brown," as she described it. Everyone would fuss over Clara and almost forget Deborah was even in the room. When her neighbors came over, they went wild over Clara, while Deborah only got a dismissive "hi." She detailed several experiences where this occurred, and she felt as if it happened just yesterday. Usually, you know you are onto something significant when the memory is more vividly clear. Sometimes, it takes more journaling to make the link.

Next, we dove into what she said to herself when this happened, what belief began to get hardwired in the synapses of her brain. She felt in these moments that she was not important, that she was not welcome. So that's what we called her wounded playlist: "I Am Not Welcome."

Now, it wasn't as if this clarity just popped into her head a second after describing her childhood wounds. She had to take some time to sit with it, to go back and view it through her childhood eyes as an adult, to write it down in her journal, and to clarify her memories of what she told herself in the instant this occurred.

Step 5: Identify the Songs of Your Playlist

Now, we need to identify songs that connect to those emotions, to that playlist title. Scroll through your music connection or Spotify to find songs that make you feel the emotions on your list, or that best represent your playlist title. Write them down. You might try searching iTunes or Spotify by putting in the exact emotion you are feeling, such as "betrayed" or "angry" to see what songs appear in your search results. I've even Googled "songs that represent anger" and come across some very interesting songs and playlist suggestions. When you have a full list of paired emotions and songs, you have your wounded playlist. Then you might want to choose one particular song that hits home the most. Which song is your anchor song, the one you might use to catch yourself when the old pattern or playlist rears its ugly head?

When you're ready to determine the songs on your initial playlist, do the following:

- Find songs that match your playlist title and corresponding emotions. It might be the lyrics or the tone of the music, but it should elicit that emotion when you hear the song.
- Determine which song affects you the most or resonates the most with your playlist title. That will be your anchor song that you can use to remind yourself when you are going down the wrong neural pathway.

- Reflect on how the songs represent the feelings instilled in you by your life experiences through the decades. What songs are annoyingly stuck in your head?

DEBORAH IDENTIFIES THE SONGS OF HER PLAYLIST

Deborah chose songs to represent her feelings of irritation, frustration, and jealousy that came from the playlist "I Am Not Welcome." She chose songs like Tom Petty and the Heartbreakers' "Don't Come Around Here No More," Kelly Clarkson's "Walk Away," and "Irreplaceable" by Beyoncé. Her anchor song was "Leave Me Lonely" by Ariana Grande, because it had the most emotional resonance for her—it best represented her playlist title. It's a song about a girl begging for love like she is begging for a dollar and is turned away just when she needs love the most. "That's exactly how I felt!" Deborah shared. "So I know this is the main song in my playlist."

DEBORAH REFLECTS ON THE IMPACT OF HER PLAYLIST ON HER LIFE

Deborah explored how her playlist continues to run in the background of her life. How many times has it influenced how she saw the world? How has this attitude colored her behavior? Certainly, it was playing out now, at work with her colleagues, as she was fighting to not be excluded from important meetings. Certainly, it was operating with her kids, and in the contentious divorce with her ex-husband. Because of the divorce, she would naturally be excluded from the activities with their father, but her playlist affected how she saw that interaction. Instead of seeing it as a way for her children to stay connected with their father, she saw it as a way for them to disconnect from her. The playlist triggered her reaction, and it made that disconnect real. She could trace it back to so many triggering moments, like the sorority rush, the neighborhood block party set for the date they knew she would be out of town, and many other seemingly "little" events that irked her. These events in her life were all playing the same songs.

Step 6: Create a New Playlist

When we stop blaming our boss, our spouse, our bodies, and other such things for our circumstances, space opens up to choose differently and see opportunities. If the problem is everyone or everything else, there's no space or ability to change. If, however, we are unwittingly listening to the same playlist on repeat and emitting the same energy, there's hope: we can change the playlist. If we created it one way, we can create it a different way. But we can't do this with guilt or shame, because that will just compound the lower-frequency emotions and cloud our ability to both see what needs to change and actually change it. We have to believe, in our core, that we have the freedom to choose—and are worthy of choosing—differently.

What does it take to feel worthy, deep down in your core? Loving yourself, your dark and light sides and all the mistakes you ever made, is the first crucial step. Yes, yes, you've heard it all before. There are songs written about this that you can't forget (thank you, Whitney Houston!). It's one thing to know it intellectually, but it's an entirely different thing to feel it emotionally. I realized I can't wait for the outside world to stop treating me unfairly. I needed to stop treating myself unfairly. More than that, I needed to *love* Susan. I needed to start to see how amazing she is! I needed to see all the talent, the empathy, the love she brings to her work and to others around her. I needed to break free of the pattern, to change the playlist, by giving Susan the love she wanted as that little toddler.

The motivation to change your playlist should be apparent. But here's what many leaders don't seem to understand: You are who you are in everything you do. You aren't a different person at home than you are at work, as much as some would like to believe otherwise. And if you haven't done the work to identify and change your playlist, *it will play you*. You may even be completely oblivious to it because you're so used to hearing it in the background. That playlist affects how you perceive the world around you, and it generates a similar pattern of emotions based on what you perceive about any given situation.

This patterning, developed in early childhood, has a direct impact on the state of your health. Or, as Donna Jackson Nakazawa says in her book *Childhood Disrupted*, "your biography becomes your biology."[2] An extensive study was done by the Centers for Disease Control and Prevention (CDC) and Kaiser Permanente to link adverse childhood events (a.k.a. trauma) to significant health issues, from obesity to autoimmune dysfunction to cancer, which can show up decades later.[3]

The initial surveys for the Adverse Childhood Experiences (ACE) Study began in 1995 and continued through 1997, with the participants followed subsequently for more than fifteen years. All results of that study are based on that original survey of 17,421 people and what was learned by following those people for so long. This was the first time that researchers had looked at the effects of several types of trauma on health, rather than the consequences of just one. What the data revealed was mind-boggling. The first shocker: there was a direct link between childhood trauma and adult onset of chronic disease, mental illness, doing time in prison, and work issues, such as absenteeism. The second shocker: about two-thirds of the adults in the study had experienced one or more types (not just incidents) of adverse childhood experiences. Of those, 87 percent had experienced two or more types. This showed that people who had an alcoholic father, for example, were likely to have also experienced physical abuse or verbal abuse. In other words, the trauma didn't usually happen in isolation. The third shocker: more adverse childhood experiences resulted in a higher risk of medical, mental, and social problems as an adult.

Of course, as mentioned before, we don't have to have a newsworthy trauma of emotional or physical abuse for deep wounds to be created in our childhoods. We don't escape our childhood without some kind of wounding. It's what we do with that wounding as an adult that makes all the difference. If you try to hold on to your cell phone's old operating system too long, you find that many of your apps don't work as effectively. The same is true with you. If you are going to upgrade the program, what's the best operating system you can develop? What new neural pathways would best serve you at this stage of your life? I realized that if I was going to get the annoying song out of my head, I needed to replace it with a new song. (This is how I do it with actual songs playing in my head as well.) What's the new song I want to hear? For me, it was recalling when I was the happiest and asking myself what emotion I was feeling. That emotion was gratitude. When I was appreciating what was right in front of me, whether it was a beautiful magnolia bloom or comfy new sheets that I slinked into at night, a feeling of joy washed over me.

Gratitude is a type of renewing emotion that emanates a higher frequency from the electromagnetic signal of your heart. The emotion of gratitude literally has a different frequency signature than a depleting emotion such as anger or grief. Not only do you feel good when you are in a state of gratitude (a "high"), but others love being around you. The higher-level frequency that the emotion of gratitude produces emanates to everyone around you.

Well, says the cynic in me (and most of the leaders I work with), "life isn't all roses and ponies." Sure, our gaze may fall on things we abhor, such as the homelessness on the San Francisco streets or the senseless police brutality that triggered a nationwide response. In my case personally, the fact that I didn't have a family, lived alone, and had no one to quarantine with when COVID-19 hit created a deep sense of loneliness and failure. I could choose depleting emotions (e.g., anger or rage), which ultimately send out a frequency that will produce more of the exact thing I didn't want, or I could choose the unexpected. I could choose the empowering response, the response that says, "I can shift my frequency and shift what gets reflected back to me."

When I was on the road to emotional recovery, I created a playlist titled "Empowerment Songs" in my iTunes library. There I put all the songs that would lift me up and remind me of the strong woman I was. It included everything from "Thank U, Next" by Ariana Grande to "No One" by Alicia Keys to "Me Too" by Meghan Trainor. I would listen to these songs as I climbed Camelback Mountain faster and faster, and they would light a fire under me and lift me up to feeling like the amazing person I am. I called it "Empowerment Songs" for simplicity, but the full statement was: *I am a badass woman! Hear me roar!*

What-if statements can be so powerful. What if I can find something to appreciate every day or even every hour? And then if that's true, what if things keep showing up for me to appreciate? And if that is possible, then what if everything is always working out for me? Because whatever shows up, I will find something to appreciate about that. What a different playlist that is from "I Am Treated Unfairly." Now my conscious and unconscious mind are training to look in a different direction where everything is working out for me, even if I can't see it in the moment.

To find your new playlist, ask yourself these questions:

- When you are happiest, what emotion are you feeling?
- What if you find ways to keep recreating that?
- What is the new frequency, the new song that can replace the old one?
- What is the what-if statement you need to keep the cynic in you from repeating lower-frequency music?

DEBORAH CREATES A NEW PLAYLIST

It would be so easy for Deborah to detail all the ways in which her colleagues or her ex were worthy of her anger and jealousy. I get it, and I'm not discounting it.

"However," I told her, "you have to know that if you are running the playlist of 'I Am Not Welcome,' you can be damn sure these characters are going to show up in the movie of your life. Can you take true ownership of the playlist?"

You can choose your response to any given situation. As much as we like to think otherwise, life will throw curve balls at us. How you handle the curve ball determines your level of happiness. For Deborah, she was able to embrace the concept. Not all clients can get there. Those who can't rise above continue to suffer, and the wounded playlist continues to run in their lives, as it did for both me and for Deborah at certain points. Sometimes it takes another deep round of suffering. What Deborah needed to do was figure out what it was that she, as that little girl, really needed from her adult self now.

"If you could go back and tell Debbie"—as she was called then—"anything, what did she most need to know?" I asked her.

"Oh!" she exclaimed. "She *is* important! She is so totally welcome and a gift to her family!"

"Wonderful!" I assured her. "And in what ways are you withholding that message from yourself today as Debbie felt it was withheld from her then? Bottom line: Where are you withholding love from yourself? What if you could feel a sense of gratitude when your kids do things with their father because you know that they will be healthier for having an involved dad in their lives? Can you imagine that? If you could choose the emotions you would like to feel when this occurs, what would they be?"

She said, "I'd like to feel like it doesn't bother me."

"Okay, great!" I said. "What emotion are you feeling instead?"

"Peaceful," she replied, "because I don't have all the responsibility of parenting."

"What else?" I asked.

"Appreciation that I have healthy kids," she said.

"Awesome!" So peace and appreciation were our anchors.

Then we created the new playlist. She started with the idea of "I Bring Peace and Appreciation." I encouraged her to create an actual playlist full of songs that brought on the feeling of peace and appreciation. Whenever she was in the car or on a walk, she should play that list and rev up the feelings of peace and appreciation. Her playlist included songs like "Thank You" by Dido, "Kind and Generous" by Natalie Merchant, "Gratitude" by Earth, Wind, and Fire, and even "(Sittin' on) The Dock of the Bay" by Otis Redding.

Then, her assignment was to get herself into a state of peace and appreciation whenever she could and then notice how welcomed she was. At first, she could name one instance of this occurring about every two weeks. There was the neighbor inviting her over for a glass of wine. Then a colleague asked her to lunch. But then it started to come faster and faster. Every day she would notice small or big ways in which she was welcomed and valued. She even chose to see the bird singing to her in the morning as a welcoming greeting. Her work was to put far more attention on these events than the old neural pathway of "I Am Not Welcome."

This was easier to do with her less contentious relationships, but what about those that were most likely to trigger the old playlist? Well, an interesting thing happened about six weeks later. Her son invited her to her grandson's Little League game but said, "Dad will be there, and I don't want you to be unhappy."

"Peace and appreciation," she said to herself and showed up with an entirely different emotional frequency. At that ball game, she felt comfortable enough to have a conversation with her ex-husband, the man she had been most angry with in the past. As this event was a success, she was invited to more and more family outings.

"I did it!" she giddily exclaimed. "I truly just feel peace and appreciation around him now. I can't believe I can say that!"

And what about work? Well, as I've said, we are who we are in everything we do. The more she showed up with the frequency of peace and appreciation, the more she felt her ideas were actually welcomed. And she started to realize that maybe she didn't need to be part of these other meetings after all; she had plenty going on in her own space to worry about. Perhaps there was a different forum to get the information she needed, a quicker way. It was then she decided to invite the colleague she was most triggered by to lunch.

"This," she said, "is going to be my real test!"

"Ah, yes!" I replied. "Life will test you to see if you really, really got a hold of this new playlist. You know what to do."

Carrying the olive branch of peace and the sunshine warmth of appreciation, they now have a regular coffee break about every other week to catch each other up on progress and make any alignment changes that are needed.

"My whole outlook has changed," she said, "and I didn't even realize it was possible."

Step 7: Devote Your Life to a More Meaningful Mission

Once you've replaced your wounded playlist with a new, more positive one, you can devote yourself to something bigger. When I can embrace gratitude for the jewel of a soul that I am, I move into a space where I don't need to control how others treat me. I don't need you to fill me up! Instead, I'm so full that I have space to clarify what really matters to me. I'm already devoted to myself, so I don't care as much if you like me. Once I stepped into this space, I could deliver the hard feedback, with love, to the executives I worked with. I could treat the billionaires as equals because in my eyes we were equals. I have nothing to be intimidated by.

And when I'm devoted to me, there is a natural hunger to expand that devotion outside myself. What am I passionate about, what is so compelling to me as a vision that I'm willing to devote my life to it? For me, the answer was having people feel empowered and loving their work. Because when you are in that state, you come home from work with gratitude in your heart to share with your family. The work I am doing to transform leaders is so that ultimately, that same little girl grows up seeing *that* human being, the empowered and grateful parent, walk through the door after work.

To find your meaningful mission, ask yourself these questions:

- If you embrace that you are "all good" or whole, what then matters to you in this world?

- What are you passionate about devoting your life to?

- Is there not a more meaningful way to spend your life than pursuing this?

DEBORAH FINDS A MEANINGFUL MISSION

This step is where what you are working on is bigger than you can imagine. And it's critical, because it provides the anchoring, the emotional charge needed to replace the old emotional charge of your playlist. In general, we as human beings like to work toward something. It gives you a reason to get up in the morning. In the past, what may have been driving you is living out the charge of having your old wounds activated and reactivated. It's similar to the glee you can see in some people's eyes when they have a juicy piece of gossip. It's not really healthy for you to tell that story and certainly not helpful for the person the gossip is about, but man do we get a charge over chatting about someone else's dirty laundry. What we need is a higher-level purpose, or it's too easy for the old playlist to insert itself back into our lives. Remember, you spent a lifetime developing those songs. The neural pathway of the old playlist is deeply grooved. If you aren't focused on a higher-level purpose, it's all too easy to revert to tending (and recreating) your childhood wounds.

And so I asked Deborah, what cause lit a fire under her? Why did she become the head of a marketing and sales organization? Why was she passionate about that? What difference was she hoping to make, knowing what she now knows about herself?

"I think I went into marketing because I wanted to articulate to people the value of something," she recalled. "In my case, it was in the medical device field. I felt like I had a special gift for doing that."

"Can you see the irony of that?" I asked. "You wanted to champion or be the mouthpiece for articulating the value of something to others."

"Yes," she looked startled. "I did that work also in the hopes that I might be valued as a talented marketer."

"And now that you get it, in your bones, that you are valued, what purpose does your work have? Is it still meaningful for you?"

"Actually, it is—in fact, more so now," she said. "I recently had a chance to talk with patients using our device and was excited about how effective it was in improving their ability to walk. Now that's important!"

When Deborah moved from doing her job (subconsciously) so that her patients and colleagues would value her to doing her job because it makes a difference in someone else's life, she became the kind of leader that finds and brings inspiration. That's the kind of leader people want to work for. And that's the kind of leader that gets even better at her core job.

13

Until You Can Hear It, You Can't Change It

For about the first ten or fifteen years of my professional life, my old playlist was at full volume. The frustration of my early career followed me into several positions, and I continued to feel left out and that I was being treated unfairly. Shortly after being held back from a promotion, I started looking for a new job. As much as I consciously wanted to avoid being like my dad, subconsciously, I was desperate to escape negative experiences and create the joyful work environment I envisioned. I was not going to be trapped in a job where I felt those emotions, and I, like most people, thought a new environment would create different emotions. If my external environment changed, my internal state would improve—or so I thought. I didn't realize what I know now: Until you deal with your wounds and address your behavior patterns, you are going to keep creating the circumstance in your life—at work and in your personal life—where the old playlist is stuck on repeat.

The reason we can't really hear the playlist on our own is because it's been playing in the background for so long. We also look for data that reinforces our current worldview. The stories we tell ourselves drive our internal perception of our lives. And what we don't always see is that we have a choice in the story we tell ourselves. Unconsciously, we are choosing to pay attention to certain data points over others.

My next job illustrates this point very well. I tell the story from two perspectives. The first perspective is the version I told myself and others about what "happened to me" for years. The second version is quite different.

What "Happened to Me"

My next job was in the quality division at a national television network as a Black Belt in the GE Six Sigma (SS) program. The company was hot to trot on the Six Sigma process, which had been instituted in other businesses with great success. Most of the GE businesses using it were in manufacturing, but GE was a firm believer that this tool (analyzing the variation in processes and reducing "error") could be applied to any business, including media. Up to this point, I hadn't had any Six Sigma training, but they wanted to hire people with consulting experience, and they promised to train us so that we could apply SS methodology in what they said was like an "internal consulting position."

I think I chose this company because I was drawn to the glamour of working within the entertainment industry. Up until then, I had been fairly bored with the industrial projects I had been doing in my previous job—researching and interviewing on such fascinating subjects as the strategic market of hydroelectric turbine engine parts. But the other thing the job had going for it was that I really liked the person who would be my manager, the leader of the quality division. He was bright and enthusiastic, had a great reputation, and was an EVP (I was only a director). I think the feeling was mutual; he seemed very impressed by my background and assured me that I would have every opportunity to develop as fast as I had in consulting. He kind of suggested he would be mentor to me, and he persuaded me that this was an opportunity not to pass up.

Given that I liked him so well, I took the job. I left Boston and moved to New York, despite a pay cut, and began my new adventure in the business side of the entertainment industry. Things started off well. I had an opportunity to work with some other SS executives in other businesses to see what I could apply to my company, and I brought back some great insights that my new boss loved.

But I started to get the impression that the rest of the organization—specifically, the sales and marketing group that we were assigned to support—wasn't so excited about this new mandated SS program. In fact, they really didn't want anybody in the quality division interfering with what they saw as their business. This made doing our jobs exceedingly difficult.

They wouldn't respond to data requests, and they wouldn't attend meetings. The only way they would participate is if my boss was directly involved. They liked him, so if a request came from him or if a meeting was held by him, they would be involved. If it came from anyone else in our group, they would just ignore us. I was concerned, but I thought I just needed to build on his reputation. The more they saw me with him, I thought, the more I would be accepted into the organization.

About a month into the job, my boss came to my office and closed the door. I knew something was up. He told me he had accepted a job with another business and would be leaving his post within two weeks. I, of course, was shocked and upset. He was one of the main reasons I had accepted the job. And since I had been there, I had seen how important he was to enabling our department to get anything done. I asked him if he knew when he brought me on board that he would be leaving, and he said, "Yes, I knew I would be leaving, but my last task was to finish hiring the rest of the team, including you. I don't know who my replacement will be, but I'm sure you guys will do okay fending for yourselves. I'm sorry, but I've got to move to greener pastures." I was flabbergasted. I had moved from a good job to a lesser-paid job in a new city essentially because of him.

As you can imagine, things got very bad for our group. The job itself was horrible. They could not find a replacement for our leader, and in the end, the resistance of the sales and marketing division won, and they decided to disband the quality group for the network. We were told that we would have to scramble to find other jobs open in the organization. I did find a job within another marketing group, but it was for a position I would have never considered after my previous job. It was several steps down from where I could have been. I was duped into this job and then betrayed by someone I admired. What a shitty experience in the corporate world!

So what was I feeling as a result of this? You guessed it: frustrated, left out, treated unfairly. I think we have all had experiences at work in which we essentially felt screwed. And you know what these stories are? They're victim stories. They are stories we tell ourselves to explain why, despite our best intentions, things didn't work out the way we wanted and now we are suffering as a result.

But there is also a very different version of this story. It was one I was forced to tell as I worked through the process of changing my own playlist. Part of that process is learning how powerful the stories we tell ourselves can be in shaping our experience. Let me share with you this version of the story.

What I Did

I was pretty disappointed with my previous job, where I hadn't received a promotion, and I hoped to find a mentor and a boss I respected and could learn from. I was also looking to move from Boston to New York because I had just gotten engaged and was eager to be with my future husband. I could have looked into just transferring with my current company to their New York office, but the truth is I was bored, felt I wasn't really valued, and wanted to try something new.

When the opportunity with the television network came up, I was blinded by what I thought would be a glamorous business—entertainment. Even though the job itself wasn't something I thought would be that exciting to me—looking at regression analysis and identifying variation in processes—I naively thought that working in an exciting industry would make up for it.

I knew that when recruiters come to you, they are generally in a selling mode. It was up to me to ask the tough questions. However, I had an image of what this job would be, and the truth is, I refused to see anything that was inconsistent with that image.

When I met with my future boss, we definitely got along, but he never made any promises that he would be my boss for any specific length of time. Did I ask him what his career plans were? No. Did I ask him what some of the challenges had been so far with the quality division and implementing SS? No. I knew I would be working closely with some of the executives in sales and marketing. Did I ask to meet with any of them, so that I could have a better understanding of their view of the role of the quality division, even before I started? No. In fact, my boss even offered for me to meet someone within sales and marketing after they gave me an offer, and I said, "There's no need. I'm already accepting it!" Once I met my boss and I liked him, I made a gut decision that this would all work out. And I ignored anything that contradicted that gut feeling.

Once I was at the company, there were lots of things I could have done to build relationships with the sales and marketing folks. But once I knew how they felt about Six Sigma, I didn't want them to find out that I hardly knew what it was—that I was just getting trained (despite my fancy title as Black Belt in Six Sigma). I chose to hide behind my boss's credentials because I didn't want to be found out for not having the knowledge I thought they thought I should have.

When my boss came to tell me he was leaving, he wanted to make sure we could talk privately. I found out later that I was the only one he met with privately. I think he really felt bad. I know how it works in corporate America: you can't announce organization changes until they give you the green light; until then, you need to do your job—which, for him, was hiring the team. I chose to make his leaving into some sort of personal betrayal and severed a relationship that could have been really helpful later in my professional life and a potential friendship in my personal life.

All in all, it turned out exactly as I created it. I didn't do my due diligence on the position, I chose it for the wrong reasons, I didn't build the relationships I needed to build, and I made my boss the fall guy.

In this version of the story, I take responsibility for what happened—for what I did to shape it and for how I reacted to what happened. At first, it seemed hard to reconcile this version with my own memories and feelings. I mean, I was wedded to my first version and believed that to be the truth. There is some truth in it, after all. But after originally telling the second version, the one in which I took full responsibility for what happened, I felt a sense of lightness come over me. I no longer felt betrayed. I didn't feel as frustrated or left out. Sure, I felt a little bad about myself for making the mistakes, but I could now see that I was just being a victim of myself, of my own self-judgment. The more I could embrace myself for making these mistakes, the easier it would be to adopt this version of the story, and the freer I would feel.

But at the time of the experience, and for years to come, I couldn't see that as a potential path. I believed that the way I experienced the events was exactly how they happened. That first version of the story just reinforced the familiar emotional experiences that my body was accustomed to and the familiar program that was running me. I never took the time to process the experience and to understand what was going on for me because I was still listening to my old playlist.

I love the adage "You can't read the label from inside the jar." It's so true. And yes, awareness is always the first step, but you can't create awareness if you become wedded to your initial version of the story. Your version of the story is related to childhood wounds that continue to surface until you fully heal them. The tough love side of me would say to myself: *You can't still be dealing with daddy issues! Haven't you done enough work on that? Get over it already!* So, while I thought I had healed these childhood wounds, the thinking that it was "all done" actually blocked me from doing further work on myself. Staying open to acknowledging that this playlist lives inside me and that it can be turned on at any time is the real awareness I've gained since then. It's not that the emotions behind the playlist go away; those neural pathways are built like a four-lane highway in my brain. It's the ability to recognize when you've gotten on the highway to hell that is the work. Just saying, "Deal with it" isn't going to work if you don't really know the insidiousness of what you are dealing with.

The epilogue to the television network job is that I did turn it into a very interesting position and got the plum title of director of marketing and business development, doing special projects for another EVP there. I also had a chance to develop the first B2B website for the company, where advertisers could go to learn more about our programming. I designed it from start to finish, and it garnered a lot of attention from the higher-ups at the company. I was quite proud of this accomplishment. It was creative and analytical at the same time. It was a hot new trend (back in the day). It required me to build relationships across the division, and it was a real, tangible work product that I could point to as a win.

I loved that I could own the outcome, felt fully engaged, and appreciated that I wasn't being micromanaged. But what made this work really exciting is that I felt I was onto something—that this type of B2B website would be highly valued and would be the future of ad sales. Looking back, I had a strong hunch that the higher-ups would value it and that I would be appreciated for it. And if I tie that into what was important to me, if I was appreciated, I wouldn't feel left out, treated unfairly, or frustrated. And, in fact, that did occur. Once we launched, overnight the website was heralded as the trend of the future. I received a lot of praise and attention for it, and I was glowing for a short couple of weeks.

As much as I wanted to, I couldn't hold on to my "baby." A higher-up VP came in and took it over to his department, since it was generating so much visibility. I'm not really sure how that happened, but you can imagine how, again, I felt frustrated. I chalked it up to "such is the political scene at the company." I was getting tired of it and began to daydream of a way out of the madness. I was soon on the job market again.

Dragons from the Past

In the book *Your Brain Is Always Listening: Tame the Hidden Dragons that Control Your Happiness, Habits, and Hang-Ups*, Daniel G. Amen outlines how our inner critic, or "dragons," as he calls them, influence our biology, psychology, social patterns, and even spiritual beliefs. Our brains are likely to listen to "dragons from the past"—critical messages that can both shut us down to our full potential and fuel us to persevere and overwork in an effort to run from the dragon.[1]

With over thirty years of brain-imaging experience, Dr. Amen categorized these dragons into several types: parent dragons, sibling and birth-order dragons, children dragons, teacher and coach dragons, peer dragons (friends, popular kids, bullies), and former-lover dragons. He notes the impact on our mental and biological health of listening to what we commonly refer to in the coaching world as "saboteurs." As he states, "Your brain is always listening to the voices of your mother or father (or mother or father figures) criticizing you or pushing you to be better. Most of us heard their words so often they became ingrained into the nerve tracks of our brain."[2]

He adds, "Our brains are always listening to the words of our parents—their guidance, expectations, approval, or disapproval." But as his categories outline, it doesn't stop there. Coach and boss dragons can also influence us and alter the course of our lives if we let them. "These dragons can be critical, hurtful, attacking, competing, and indifferent, or they can be encouraging, positive, comforting, and engaged."[3]

Looking back, I think my drive to excel and to achieve was influenced both by my mother and father dragons. Not a day goes by that my mother doesn't outline all the things she accomplished in a day. Even at eighty-six, she details to me how she did laundry, watered the plants, organized the office, and so on. It's abundantly clear that she doesn't feel good unless she is always busy and accomplishing something. Of course, that messaging was hardwired into me, and what I made it mean was that "I am a good person if I achieve success." And if I am not achieving success, despite working hard, then something must be "unfair" in the system. My father further reinforced this dragon by giving me praise and admiration if I did well. But if I didn't, I was ignored, criticized, or—even worse—ridiculed. Only by becoming aware of these dragons and slaying them could I move on to feeling truly happy. Forgive the mixed metaphor, but changing my playlist helped me slay the dragons.

Catching Negative Thought Patterns

In the book *Cognitive Behavioral Therapy Made Simple: 10 Strategies for Managing Anxiety, Depression, Anger, Panic, and Worry*, author Seth Gillihan highlights how our negative thought patterns can dupe us into believing a situation is far worse than it is. He writes about how important it is to step back and listen to what you are telling yourself to catch lies and half-truths—a practice that is much easier to spot in other people than in our own thinking. "For something that can't be seen, heard, or measured, thoughts have incredible power," he writes, "and we can use our thought patterns to either tear us down or build us up."[4]

One suggestion Gillihan gives to catch the negative thought patterns that tear us down is to imagine what we would say to our best friend if they were in a similar situation. After a car accident, would we berate our friend for making a mistake and blowing through the stop sign when we can clearly see they are upset? Unlikely. And yet that is exactly what we do to ourselves when these negative thought patterns take hold. "Unfortunately we tend to assume our thoughts reflect an impartial take on reality," but that couldn't be further from the truth.[5]

To detect when a negative thought pattern is at play, your emotions are your guide. If you feel a sudden shift and experience depleting emotions (a jolt of anger, seething resentment) and you feel stuck in those emotions, chances are a negative thought pattern has taken hold to keep that emotion activated. Gillihan suggests that we keep in mind the following when identifying thought patterns: give yourself the space to check in with how you are feeling (acknowledge versus resist); be aware that thoughts may come in the form of images or impressions rather than words; and look for cognitive distortions that may be driving the negative thought pattern. Gillihan explains that cognitive distortions, or thinking errors, include the following:

- Black and white thinking: seeing things in extreme terms
- *Should*ing: thinking the way we want things to be is the way they ought to be
- Overgeneralizations: believing that one instance applies to every situation
- Catastrophizing: thinking a situation is much worse than it is
- Discounting the positive: minimizing evidence that contradicts the negative thought pattern
- Predictions: making assumptions on the future with scant information
- Mind reading: assuming we know what someone else is thinking
- Personalization: thinking of events that have nothing to do with us are actually about us
- Entitlement: expecting to reach a certain outcome based on our actions

- Outsourcing happiness: giving outside sources the final say on our emotions

- False helplessness: thinking we have less power than we actually do

- A false sense of responsibility: thinking we have more power than we actually do[6]

In cognitive behavioral therapy, you work to identify the interpretations you have made between an event and your feelings about it. Gillihan suggests that you create a chart that has the event that affected you in one column, what you told yourself about that event in a second column, and the resulting feelings in a third. You may even create a fourth column that identifies the resulting behavior. Jotting down the second column, you will see some of the cognitive distortions listed above. This will help bring to consciousness that a negative thought pattern has taken hold.[7]

Once you see it, you can change it. One way to do this is to write down evidence that supports the belief and in equal measure write down evidence that doesn't. Is there anything your initial belief ignored? Or think about what you would tell a friend in a similar situation. What would you point out that they may have ignored? The main thing is to look for thinking errors. Likely, at least one of Gillihan's cognitive distortions is at play. Finally, create a more helpful and accurate way of seeing the event. What would be a more useful perspective to take on the situation? Then notice the resulting impact on your feelings about the situation over time, and notice the effect of this shift on you.

This process is taken a step further when we explore core beliefs that shape our worldview. As Gillihan states, "Our negative automatic thoughts are not random."[8] If we analyze our thought patterns, we'll find themes occurring again and again, which will vary for each of us. Our responses to triggering situations will reveal our own core beliefs.

Having a different core belief would create a very different set of experiences for any given leader. Paying attention to what you think others believe to be true about you can help you identify negative core beliefs. This negative core belief is your playlist, and its songs are on repeat in the background of your life.

As Gillihan explains, to shift the negative core belief, we need to start to give our attention to evidence in our lives that contradicts the belief. Gratitude practices and daily journaling for recording things that go well, he suggests, can help shift your mindset.[9] I did this, and it was helpful, but it didn't seem to stick to break the pattern. But I discovered that combining journaling, gratitude practice, and music got me there.

Making Beautiful Music Together

In the book *This Is Your Brain on Music*, rocker-turned-neuroscientist Daniel Levitin explores the connection between music and the mind. He outlines why we emotionally attach to the music we listen to as teenagers and how insidious jingles get stuck in our heads. He confirms statements made by Brainfacts.org that musical activity involves nearly every part of our brain and nearly every neural subsystem. Levitin explains, "At a deeper level, the emotions we experience in response to music involve structures deep in the primitive, reptilian regions of the cerebellar vermis and the amygdala—the heart of emotional processing in the cortex."[10]

He goes on to say:

The brain goes through a rapid neural development after birth, continuing for the first few years of life. During this time, new neural connections are forming more rapidly than at any other time in our lives, and during our midchildhood years, the brain starts to prune these connections, retaining only the most important and most needed ones. This becomes the basis for our understanding of music and, ultimately, the basis for what we like in music, what music moves us, and how it moves us. This is not to say we can't learn to appreciate new music as adults, but basic structural elements are incorporated into the very wiring of our brains when we listen to music early in our lives. Music, then, can be thought of as a type of perceptual illusion in which our brain imposes structure and order on a sequence of sounds. Just how this structure leads us to experience emotional reactions is part of the mystery of music.[11]

Music directly connects with your brain and your memories. This is why our new playlist allows us to shift our actions and our reactions. Changing our playlists allows us to literally change our minds.

The Enlightened Leader

Ultimately it's my hope that all of us can learn these lessons so we can move forward together in our society toward a more evolved, more loving, and more successful future. Singing in unison, emanating a frequency that is a new and more vibrant tune, we can each contribute to a better world by doing the work to become better leaders. I'd like to create a community of executives who support each other in shifting from wound to purpose.

I launched a YouTube channel and a podcast called *The Enlightened*

Executive to help create that community and inspire others on their path to enlightened leadership. Here I share other groundbreaking techniques to help enhance your personal and leadership effectiveness with candid, conversational, and in-depth interviews of other enlightened leaders or founders of extraordinary programs. I believe that we all have the potential to be visionaries—to be a game changer in how we lead and what we create in the world. Our personal evolution will spark our leadership evolution.

If this book spoke to you (and if you are reading at this point, there must have been some chord that was struck!), I encourage you to join our community. You can do this on SusanDrumm.com, with our EL Mastermind, or you can subscribe to the *Enlightened Leader* channel. There is strength in numbers and power in cultivating an orchestra rather than trying to be a one-person band.

Right now, I'd like for you to think of all the leaders you've worked for in your career. You may even want to write down their names—the bad leaders, the mediocre ones, and, if you are blessed to have had one, the more enlightened leaders. For the poor and mediocre ones, now see if you can identify, based on their behavior, which of the wounds we've discussed may have been driving their leadership style. Were they fighting for safety, or were they always pursuing perfection?

Now contrast that with the best leader you have ever worked for. Who was that person, and how were they different? What made your experience working with them more inspiring and development-oriented than all the rest? What difference were you able to make as a result of their leadership?

Imagine a day when the more enlightened, the more conscious, leader is more of the norm than the unicorn. Imagine if most of your bosses were like the best leader you ever worked for. What would be possible for you, your colleagues, and the mission of the organization?

Now imagine you are that enlightened leader. How would your own leadership affect you, your family, and your organization?

Changing your playlist is not only possible, but I believe it is imperative that we take this mission on. We know change is possible; we know about the neuroplasticity of the brain. So let's start harnessing our ability to make these changes and free ourselves from the tethers of the wounding of our ancestors.

To help you determine which wound may be yours, we created a simple quiz to give you a head start in your own exploration. Visit www.susandrumm.com and take the free Enlightened Leadership assessment. This is a simple quiz designed to point in the direction of your wound, not to be a definitive answer to it (which would be fairly unlikely in a seven-question quiz). As you read your results, look to see what resonates and what doesn't, and then compare with the other wounds we have identified. We welcome your feedback and suggestions to continue to level up the quality of the results.

Pop, pop, it's showtime, it's showtime: let's find that twenty-four-karat magic in the air and play the melody that transforms our human experience and our leadership.

Notes

INTRODUCTION

1. A. H. Maslow, "A Theory of Human Motivation," *Psychological Review* 50, no. 4 (1943): 370–396.

2. Learning in Action, "Heal the Divide Mission," accessed April 11, 2022, https://learninginaction.com.

CHAPTER 1

1. Donna Jackson Nakazawa, *Childhood Disrupted: How Your Biography Becomes Your Biology, and How You Can Heal* (New York: Atria Books, 2015), 28.

2. Nakazawa, *Childhood Disrupted*, 30–32.

3. Nakazawa, *Childhood Disrupted*, 35.

4. Nakazawa, *Childhood Disrupted*, 36.

5. Nakazawa, *Childhood Disrupted*.

6. Bessel van der Kolk, *The Body Keeps the Score: Brain, Mind, and Body in the Healing of Trauma* (New York: Penguin, 2015), 21.

7. van der Kolk, *The Body Keeps the Score*, 44.

8. van der Kolk, *The Body Keeps the Score*, 45.

9. van der Kolk, *The Body Keeps the Score*, 62.

CHAPTER 2

1. Joel Beckerman and Tyler Gray, *The Sonic Boom: How Sound Transforms the Way We Think, Feel, and Buy* (Boston: Mariner Books, 2015), 133.

2. Jessica Guo, "Music: A Full Brain Workout," BrainFacts.org, November 9, 2020, https://www.brainfacts.org/thinking-sensing-and-behaving/hearing/2020/music-a-full-brain-workout-110920.

3. Guo, "Music."

4. Kiminobu Sugaya and Stephanie Merchant, "How to Approach Alzheimer's Disease Therapy Using Stem Cell Technologies," *Journal of Alzheimer's Disease* 15, no. 2 (2008), doi:10.3233/JAD-2008-15209.

5. Dementia Care Central, "Music Therapy: How It Enriches the Lives of Persons with Dementia and Reduces Behavioral Challenges," June 5, 2019, https://www.dementiacarecentral.com/caregiverinfo/music-as-therapy/.

6. Carnegie Hall, "Why Making Music Matters: Music and Early Childhood Development," accessed April 11, 2022, https://www.carnegiehall.org/Explore/Articles/2020/12/09/Why-Making-Music-Matters.

7. "Jar of Hearts," *Wikipedia*, April 10, 2022, https://en.wikipedia.org/wiki/Jar_of_Hearts.

CHAPTER 3

1. All names and circumstances are fictionalized but inspired by actual clients and events.

CHAPTER 6

1. Timothy Ferriss, *The 4-Hour Workweek* (New York: Harmony, 2009).

CHAPTER 12

1. For more about Learning in Action, see its website, at https://learninginaction.com.

2. Donna Jackson Nakazawa, *Childhood Disrupted: How Your Biography Becomes Your Biology, and How You Can Heal* (New York: Atria Books, 2015), 29.

3. Nakazawa, *Childhood Disrupted*, 97.

CHAPTER 13

1. Daniel G. Amen, *Your Brain Is Always Listening: Tame the Hidden Dragons That Control Your Happiness, Habits, and Hang-Ups* (Carol Stream, IL: Tyndale Refresh, 2021), 16.

2. Amen, *Your Brain Is Always Listening*, 81.

3. Amen, *Your Brain Is Always Listening*, 94.

4. Seth Gillihan, *Cognitive Behavioral Therapy Made Simple: 10 Strategies for Managing Anxiety, Depression, Anger, Panic, and Worry* (Berkeley, CA: Althea Press, 2018), 52.

5. Gillihan, *Cognitive Behavioral Therapy*, 54.

6. Gillihan, *Cognitive Behavioral Therapy*, 57.

7. Gillihan, *Cognitive Behavioral Therapy*, 58.

8. Gillihan, *Cognitive Behavioral Therapy*, 71.

9. Gillihan, *Cognitive Behavioral Therapy*, 176.

10. Daniel Levitin, *This Is Your Brain on Music: The Science of a Human Obsession* (New York: Plume/Penguin, 2007), 86.

11. Levitin, *This Is Your Brain on Music*, 109.